The Master Arpeggio System for Jazz Improvisation V2.0

Expanded Edition

The Master Arpeggio System for Jazz Improvisation V2.0 - Expanded Edition

Second Edition

Copyright © 2022 by Dennis Roberts

ISBN: 979-8-9872566-0-2 (paperback)

ISBN: 979-8-9872566-1-9 (ebook)

Library of Congress Control Number: 2021901243

Formatting done by Trisha Fuentes
Cover design by Rachel Bostwick
Cover art: Md.Shafique Mahmud, designermdshafi at Fiverr.com

Printed in the United States

Published by MAS4JI.com
Bennington, VT

The Master Arpeggio System for Jazz Improvisation V2.0

Expanded Edition

Dennis Roberts

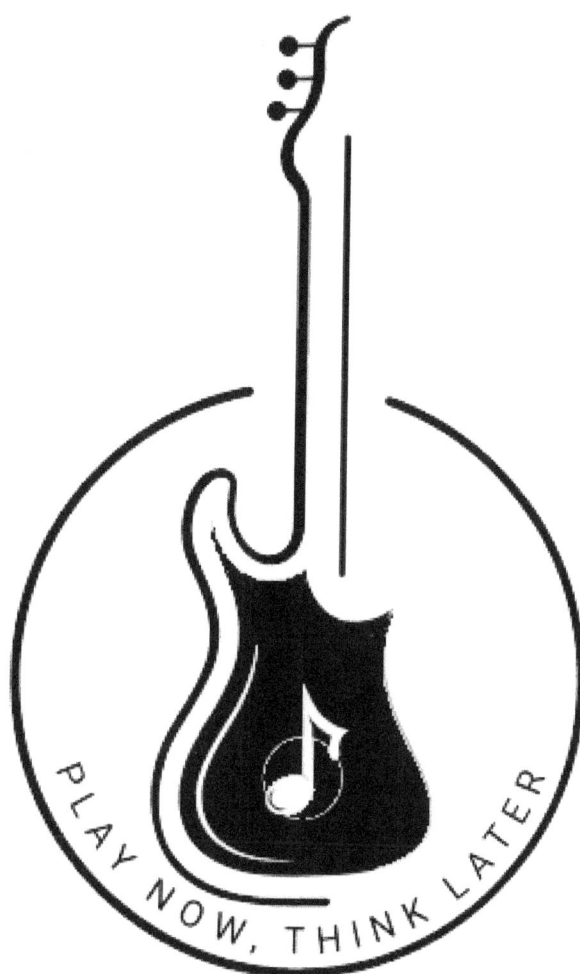

PLAY NOW, THINK LATER

MAS4JI

For a link to download audio examples and for all correspondence, please contact the author at

DRoberts@mas4ji.com or **drrobts@gmail.com**
or look up **MAS4JI** or author's name on
SoundCloud

Contents

Foreword

"The shortest distance between two points is a straight line"

Dennis Roberts' approach follows a clear path that develops the ability to speak and understand the musical language. The Master Arpeggio System for Jazz Improvisation is a system that, bit by bit, incrementally teaches us how to organize our musical thoughts. By guiding the process in such an organized manner, we never lose clarity of focus and are able to *work smarter, not harder.* Moreover, we are able to learn quickly and effectively in a fashion that allows us to fully internalize our material of study. His approach follows a conceptual straight line that finds the shortest distance to musical fluency.

There is endless musical content to learn; this boundlessness is overwhelming, and it is easy for our process to become scattered and inefficient. Dennis understands the importance of organizing our approach to learning. By devising a system that is grounded in fundamental concepts, he has found a way to approach learning in a clear manner that guides us through understanding the musical language.

To speak fluently and naturally, we do not fixate on underlying components of language during the process of speech. Likewise, to improvise fluently, we must be able to tacitly understand musical mechanics while actively creating sound. Dennis' system catalogs key concepts in a manner that can be understood quickly, retained, and drawn upon automatically to make music. This book refines our understanding of essential musical topics so that we can create informed music as freely as possible.

Organization of our learning process is integral to our success. Unfortunately, it is often overlooked and can become a hindrance to our development. Fortunately, Dennis Roberts understands this and has created a straight line that guides us towards musical fluency.

Alex Goodman
Montreux Jazz Festival International Guitar Competition, 1st Prize and Audience Choice Award Winner 2014; JUNO nominee Contemporary Jazz Album of the Year
https://www.alexgoodmanmusic.com/

Introduction

Improvisation is the art of spontaneous composition. In jazz, this spontaneous composition uses a variety of techniques that give the jazz language its unique sound and style. However, when learning to speak this language, things can get very academic, full of musician jargon and music education vernacular that can quickly become overwhelming and leave the new jazz guitarist overthinking their every move. On the other end of the spectrum, improvisation can also get very philosophical and esoteric, spoken of in abstract terms like an insider secret.

It's all too easy to get bogged down in endless exercises as we try to learn the jazz alphabet so we can form sentences and paragraphs using this seemingly complex (at first glance) language. You hear about target tones, guide tones and voice leading, superimposing triads, arpeggios and scales, quartal arpeggios, chromaticism and so much more. Studying these exhaustive subjects can become a labor-intensive journey through a seemingly endless maze where the goal is often elusive.

The book you're holding in your hand presents a very unique and innovative approach, almost a **quick start** method for improvising jazz and fusion style lines. Very significantly, this is not a book on how to play jazz. It does not teach you how to solo in the specific styles of bebop, hard bop, post-bop or any other kind of bop. Instead, it's a flexible method that teaches you how to access the general jazz language without all the jargon and vernacular by using some simple diagrams, brief explanations, and demonstrations of the ideas being presented. I strive to put potentially unfamiliar terms in italics so the student can look them up on their own to better understand what we're learning, but I keep these to a minimum.

Again, this book is about **improvising**, the true heart of jazz and fusion. It's about learning how to generate great sounding lines in the moment, almost out of thin air, based on a method that, once learned, allows you to use the sounds professional jazz musicians use without having to think too much about what, where and when to play a technique because you can mix and match these ideas almost at random and sound good. It's almost—but not quite—a color by numbers method, except that no specific colors are assigned to any particular numbers, leaving you free to color however you like and create your own sonic landscape and develop your own sound and style.

The Master Arpeggio System for Jazz Improvisation (MAS4JI) is not reinventing the wheel, it's simply reorganizing the information and presenting it from a slightly different angle than it's traditionally taught so that it's easier and faster to learn and apply. MAS4JI takes a more holistic approach using a memory aid and learning technique called **chunking** to put a lot of useful information at your fingertips quickly, then uses key center playing to apply it. It also uses something we guitarists just love: patterns!

After we learn these relatively few chunks of critical information—the master arpeggios—we learn how to manipulate and embellish them in a progressive way where we build on what we've already learned step-by-step until we're using all the same essential ideas as the jazz greats without getting too deep into the technical music theory.

The idea here is to **play more, think less**, without worrying too much about all the theory and indepth analysis of what we're doing. Really, we just need to hear it, get it, and be on our way, up and running with ideas we can immediately use. We want to get playing and expressing ourselves as soon as possible, using our creativity and imagination. We can learn all the theory and analyze everything later if we want. Right now, we just want to play and enjoy it.

So, who is this book for? It's for motivated, self-taught guitarists who want to move quickly into the jazz and fusion realm and improvise great lines using their intuition without paying the high costs of tuition. It's for guitarists who want to access cool jazz sounds to use with their existing blues, rock, metal, or progressive playing styles. It's for music students who have recitals coming up and want to jumpstart their improvisation skills so they can hit one out of the park. It's for teachers and instructors that want a system that's very easy to teach and produces great results with less frustration in shorter time.

How to use this book: This book is organized in a series of progressive studies that's meant to be learned in the order it's presented. In the first chapter we lay the crucial foundation and the chapters that follow are very carefully and deliberately organized to build on that foundation in logical steps so the information can be learned and applied very quickly. Skipping around completely defeats the purpose and effectiveness of the course and the accelerated learning curve is lost.

If you stick with it, you'll see dramatic results in only six months or less, and in a year, your playing can be transformed into something remarkably different than it was when you started. This system is teaching a concept that is designed to lead to a series of "Aha!" Eureka moments as the light bulbs flash and everything comes together so you can begin merging it with your existing playing style to create something that's uniquely you. It's a journey of discovery that teaches you how to teach yourself.

It's my sincere hope that guitarists will have a similar experience to my own. I was the very first student of this method, which came to me in a flash of inspiration while I was lying in bed sick with a fever one summer day. It's a deceptively simple system so don't overthink it. I hope you grow by leaps and bounds and that it takes your playing to new heights and new levels of spontaneous expression and freedom to improvise cool jazz and fusion style lines.

Chapter One:
The Master Arpeggios

Introducing the Master Arpeggio

The master arpeggio is an expansive arpeggio that spans all six strings of the guitar and contains a sequence of notes that has a different version ascending than it does when descending. All of the primary notes you need for soloing are contained within the master arpeggio and it will be the foundation for everything that follows. Improvising great jazz style lines comes from manipulating and embellishing the master arpeggios. Lines will flow easily from this form because it is intervallic rather than scalar, so it's inherently melodic, more visual on the fretboard, and easy to work with.

The Major Master Arpeggio

Pictured below is the root position for the major master arpeggio (we'll refer to the master arpeggios as maps, which sounds much better than marps). Most of the examples in this book will be based in the guitar friendly key of A major for relative ease of learning and consistency. Likewise, we'll keep the progressions pretty simple while we learn this method and Amaj7 will be our root (I) chord.

The first image below is the root position A major map as a fretboard diagram, followed by the basic ways to learn and play it in musical notation and tablature, plus the suggested fingering. For the fretboard diagrams, the horizontal lines represent the strings, with low E on the bottom and high E on top. The vertical lines represent the frets. The white and black dots are notes on the fretboard. Numbers above the diagram correspond with fret numbers or dot inlays on the guitar neck.

When you learn this map, you can play the black dots (notes) ascending and the white dots (notes) descending, then play it the opposite way: white dots ascending and then black dots descending. Likewise, you can play this map from the top, descending and then ascending, starting alternately on either black or white dots.

Your goal is to be able to play this map in all the ways mentioned above. Play it frontward, backward, inside and out, starting from the top and ending on any note anywhere in the pattern. You need to be able to do this with all ten of the maps in this chapter. These ten maps will provide the foundation for most of the material to follow, which you'll use for improvising jazz lines in any style over typical basic major jazz chord progressions.

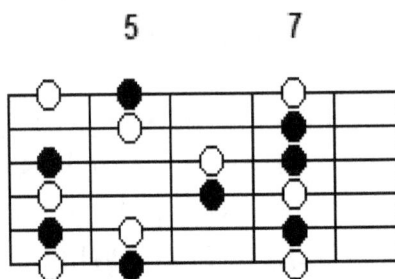

A major root position

3 Then . . .

4 And . . .

It's important to note that none of the examples in this chapter are exercises. Rather, they're simply devices to help get you started memorizing the maps and learning them in relation to one another. You need to get these under your fingers before we move on.

Tips for Learning and Memorization

The ten maps are essentially based off of a learning and memorization technique called "chunking," which quickly puts more ready-to-use information at our fingertips and bypasses a lot of the general learning curve going into improvising jazz style lines. It uses something we guitarists just love: patterns. Ideally, you want to learn these maps as ten big chunks of information. However, it might help to break them down into some smaller chunks at first to help you learn and memorize them faster.

One way to do this is to take the six strings and mentally divide them into two sets of three strings and play the maps right through all six strings while seeing and feeling the shapes at first in sets of three strings until they merge seamlessly together and you can see and feel the entire larger map pattern with ease.

3   5   7

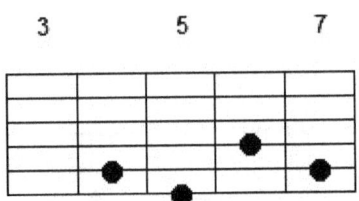

A major root position

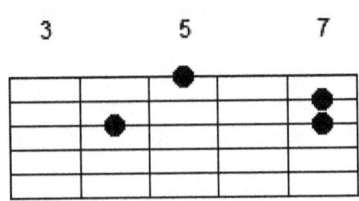

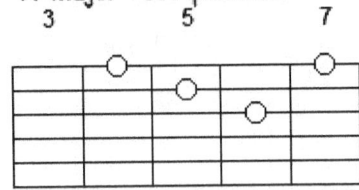

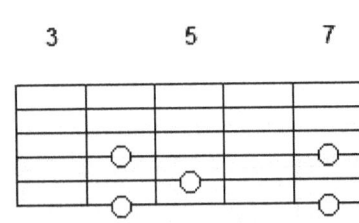

3   5   7

A major root position

3   5   7

A major root position

3   5   7

A major root position

To recap play through the entire map, but feel the smaller shapes falling under your fingers until you don't need to think about or feel them anymore and you're playing and feeling the complete map with ease. Initially learning the maps is the biggest learning curve in the MAS4JI.

Don't rely on these smaller chunks like a crutch, but use them as an aid to speed up the learning process. It's important to know each of these maps well before we begin exploring what we can do with them, so we first need to be able to visualize and play them whole before we look at the parts. Very soon you're going to go fast and far and get a lot of mileage out of this small fleet of vehicles.

Play the map frontward and backward, ascending and descending, and practice switching between playing the white dots and the black dots randomly. For example, you could play four black dots ascending, then move down to the next white dot and descend with three of those, then ascend from the next black dot above or below, playing four or five in a row, then move to the next white dot and continue ascending. You can even play as few as two white or black dots before switching to the other and you can play up a fragment of the map in white or black dots and pivot off of one, playing back down the same dots before switching off again, like we often do with rock and metal style arpeggios. This is a great thing to practice mindfully and focused, but also great to do while watching TV. You want to be able to move around within these arpeggios without even thinking.

Just remember, you want to be able to play the map as an entire unit before you begin breaking it down. I can't stress that enough because the system is specifically designed for efficiency and fast learning. It's very important not to put the cart in front of the horse or you could put someone's eye out (to mix metaphors).

Introducing the Altered Master Arpeggio

The major map has a dance partner: the altered map. These two work together a lot in jazz. The altered map complements the major map in this sonic tango. In the key of A major, our altered map is based on the dominant V chord, especially when altered (but don't let a straight V stop you!), so we'll use an E altered map. In the key of A major, Amaj7 is the I chord and E7 is the V (or V7) chord. For more information, look up the Roman Numeral System for music theory online. The diagram below introduces the E altered map and displays it in relation to the A major map we just learned.

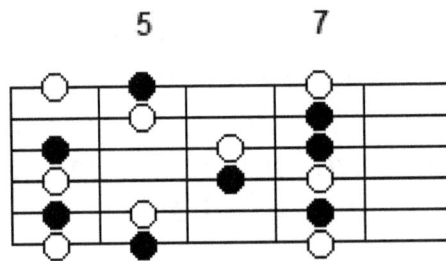

A major root position

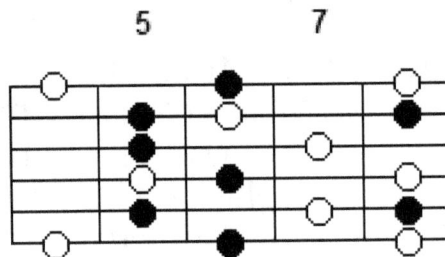

E altered from 3rd/b4

Tips for Learning and Memorization

Learn, memorize, and practice this map the same way as you did the major map: frontward, backward, inside and out, beginning and ending anywhere within, breaking it into smaller three-string chunks at first if it helps speed up the process.

Now we want to connect these two maps together because they will frequently work closely with one another, especially while we're learning this method. So the next step is to begin moving between the major map and the altered map. To begin, simply play ascending through the major map and then descending with the altered map, doing so in all combinations: ascending black dots in one, descending black dots in the other; ascending white dots, descending black dots. Do the same descending and ascending.

When you have that down, you also want to be able to switch around anywhere within them, moving freely back and forth between these two maps. Experiment switching freely between the two until you can do so very comfortably and without losing your way. See the bigger picture: two linked master arpeggios.

Here are some examples demonstrating how to learn these.

6
A major
E altered
A major

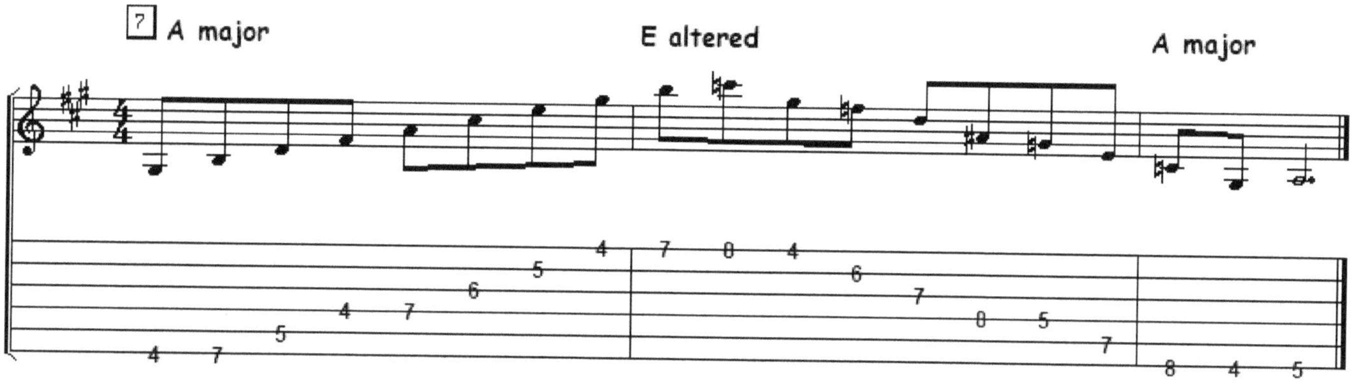
7
A major
E altered
A major

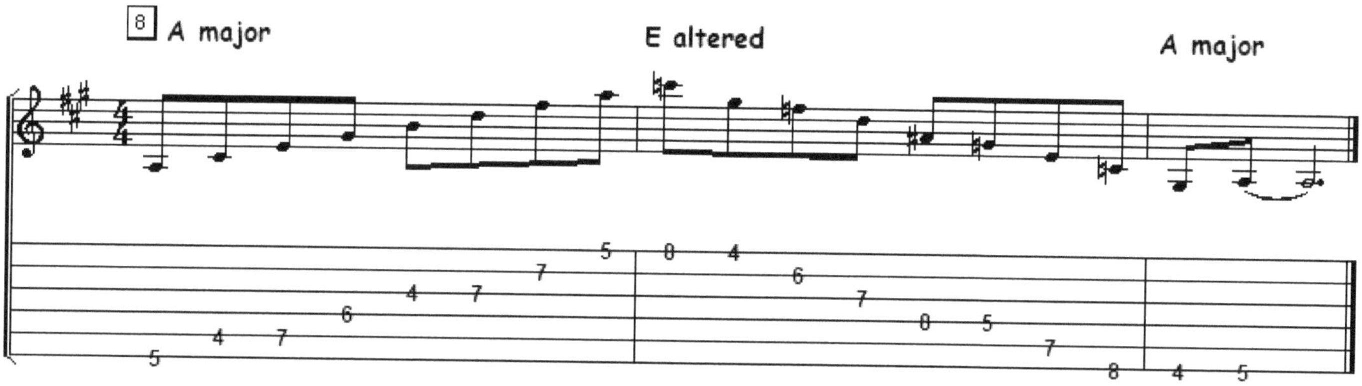
8
A major
E altered
A major

9
A major
E altered
A major

The Ten Master Arpeggios

Altogether, there are ten maps. These will become the bread and butter of your jazz phrasing and improvisation in this book. This chapter presents the main learning curve of the entire method, but once you have it down you'll be ready to fly with the eagles in no time because everything else that follows will take off from this launch pad and this concept. Most of what you have left to learn here will be based on these ten maps.

After you've learned the first two maps (major and altered in one position), you want to learn each new major map, then each new altered map, then the two as a pair, all using the learning, memorization and practice techniques we set out for the first two. Do this until you've learned all ten.

Your goal is to picture each map pair as an intertwined unit that works together complementarily. In time, with practice and familiarity, all of the maps will blend together into a single form that's linked over the fretboard without boundaries, one arpeggio flowing through the next, moving into and through the one above and below it so you can move in any direction you choose in the moment.

Examples 10 through 19 demonstrate the ten master arpeggios in their respective pairs.

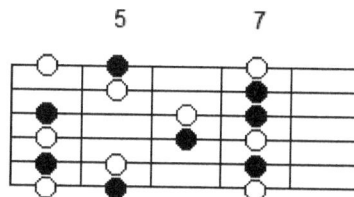

A major root position

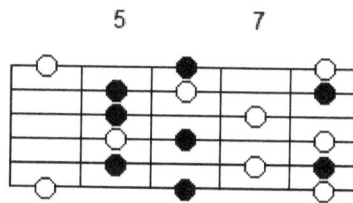

E altered from 3rd/b4

10

11

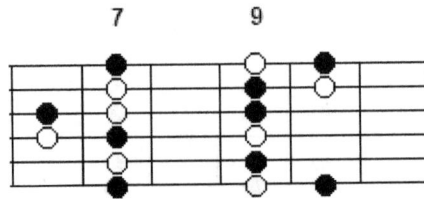

A major from 2nd

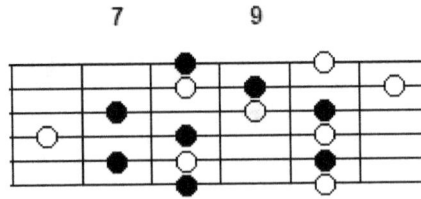

E altered from b6/b13 (#5)

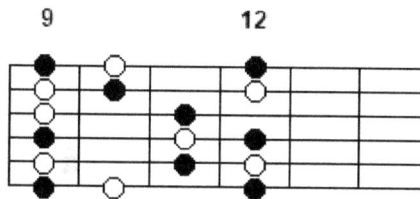

A major from 3rd

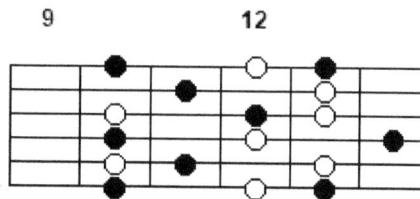

E altered from b7th

14

15

17

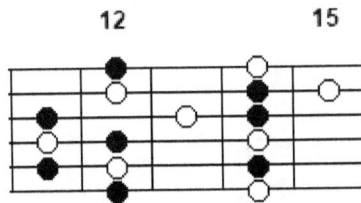

A major from 5th

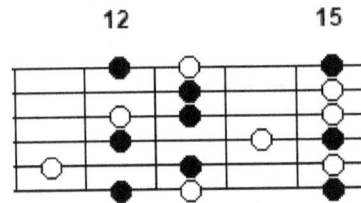

E altered from root

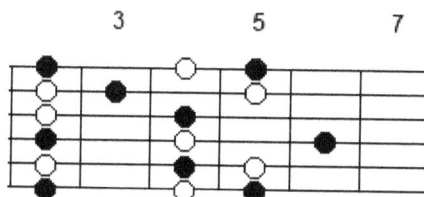

A major from 6th

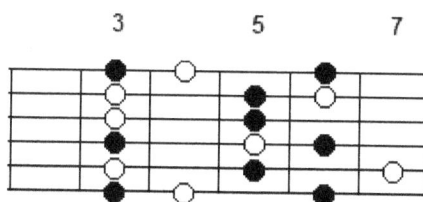

E altered from b3/#9

18

19

19

Some Brief Notes

That's it: the toughest part! For those who are curious, the maps are based on a modified version of the CAGED system. There are some stretches for your hand, but they're not too hard and the modifications help when using the maps as pairs and moving between them. Just remember to relax into them. I find it easier to place my pinky and reach with my index, at least at first.

I don't use three-note-per-string scales to form the master arpeggios because these maps chunk the information into fewer units and the maps that are formed with the three-note patterns are more difficult to play comfortably. Again, you can adapt and use everything here in your playing however you like as it all comes together for you.

Once you've learned and assimilated the concept here, you can modify and use the information any way you like because you will likely start using your own blues and rock licks and techniques with this system very soon as things click into place. Also, you'll fragment the maps more and more and alter them to fit your needs. It's all part of the process.

Let's recap our learning and memorization method:

- Black dots ascending, white dots descending.

- White dots ascending, black dots descending.

- Black dots descending, white dots ascending.

- White dots descending, black dots ascending.

- Play randomly up and down through portions of each map, switching back and forth between black and white dots every three notes or more, pivoting off notes, changing direction, moving around until you're very comfortable and familiar with the pattern, even using as few as two notes at times.

- Play randomly up and down between map pairs, switching back and forth between black and white dots every three notes or more, pivoting off notes, changing direction, moving around until you're very comfortable and familiar with this bigger pattern, again using as few as two notes at times.

- Start being musical as soon as you begin getting comfortable; melodic phrases are easy with MAS4JI because of the intervallic nature of the maps.

For our final examples, here's a snapshot of what just a few moments of practice might look like as you randomly play around in the major map, followed by playing between the major and altered maps. Notice how there's no real pattern or direction, nor is it particularly musical. That's because this is not an exercise; it's orientation. You learn the maps ascending and descending and then switch to randomly moving around through them until it becomes second nature so you can move around freely and without limits.

Notice how seemingly random the lines are already at this early stage, how I change direction, pivot off of notes, retrace my steps, and just wander around in an exploratory nature. No two "practice" sessions with the maps should be the same because repetitious exercises are not necessary with this method. If anything, they're counterproductive and will hold you back from making fast progress. Learn to navigate the maps freely and we'll begin using them to improvise lines quickly.

Fingerings are included throughout the book to demonstrate how I set myself up to move vertically and horizontally through positions. This becomes increasingly important as we start to really travel around the fretboard while improvising, moving through the maps as we play. This is based on how great professional players move between and through positions on the guitar neck.

Chapter Two:
How to Use Our Maps

The Push and Pull

Jazz improvisation—and music in general—is all about the interplay of consonance and dissonance, tension and resolution. At the heart of this method, the altered map is where you create tension and the major map is where you resolve it. When soloing, you're always moving from a place of relatively low tension, where the music is relatively consonant, into a place of greater tension, building interest and creating motion, passing through that sound and back toward a place of rest. This push and pull between these two sounds is the tightrope you want to walk like a pro.

When phrasing, you form sentences containing statements, questions and answers, and paragraphs of musical dialog that tell a story. The dissonance is like conflicts that need to be resolved to varying degrees as the story unfolds, builds to a climax, and finally draws to a conclusion. Tension gives momentum to your lines and solos as you create a tug-o-war between consonance and dissonance.

As you tell your story, you might raise your voice and shout, then lean in and whisper, then throw a startling question at your audience, answering it in a confident and reassuring voice. You might pause for effect and leave the audience hanging on your words before you continue. With each phrase and solo you get to weave your tale and tell your story, drawing the listener along with you.

Essentially, the major map is where your start your story and the altered map is where you introduce tension and make the audience lean in closer with increased interest until you resolve it back to your major map. This fundamental principle will always apply as we develop this concept.

You want to keep your listeners guessing and avoid being too predictable. You're like a guide leading hikers through a forest. They're following you and you're walking along a clear path through the trees. Suddenly, you veer off into the woods, not too far, walking parallel to the path for a few moments. Your guests wonder, "Where is he going?!" Then you step back out of the woods and onto the path and everyone breathes a sigh of relief, "Oh, there he is!" You do this repeatedly on your journey so it keeps them on their toes and attentive.

How to Practice and Develop Your Ear

We're going to avoid repetitious exercises, but we will practice the maps in an exploratory fashion to discover their sounds. The first—and simplest—way to begin practicing this material is to play through the altered map and chromatically resolve it to notes within the major map just above it.

Next, do the same, but try to resolve the altered map to notes in the major map below it. Doing this will help you quickly link the maps in an interlacing pattern that covers the entire neck of the guitar and really opens up the fretboard. We've already been practicing for this, but now we want to be musical and create intelligent lines with strong melodies and rhythms.

If we run with the metaphor ball again, we can think of each individual map and map pair as a street map for a city or town and there are many routes you can take through the town to get from place to place. Our maps link together to form a visual and sonic map of the region that gives you a bigger picture still, where you can travel the highways and byways to get from city to city and town to town. The Master Arpeggio System is your GPS, showing the way so you don't get hopelessly lost and end up on some dead end dirt road in the backwoods in the middle of nowhere.

You want to be able to play the notes from anywhere in the altered map and resolve them chromatically anywhere within the major map to develop fluency toggling between the two. Play black dots, switch to white dots, moving freely in any direction with them. Swing your 8th notes, try straight 8s, play triplets and quarter note triplets, and whatever rhythms you're comfortable playing. Mix them up and use dynamics. This is your journey.

Be creative and musical right from the start now. This is an extension of where we left off in the last chapter; the next step. Arpeggios and triads (when you're playing in white or black dots) are inherently melodic and lend themselves to nice melodic phrasing. At this stage, we're just focusing on breaking maps into fragments and moving around within them and between them, dividing them into smaller parts while visualizing the bigger picture: the map we're drawing our ideas from. We're familiarizing ourselves with all the streets and getting to know the area we're traveling through, getting from point A to point B by various routes and knowing where we are in relation to our environment at all times.

Aim for the Gaps

To help you recognize what you're listening for, play the lines below and hear how the altered map resolves into the major map so the line sounds complete, finished, over and done. These brief lines each use the same notes from the altered map to resolve to various neighboring notes in the major map on just the first string. Any notes in the altered map can resolve chromatically to any notes of the major map. The gaps in the altered map are generally notes you can resolve to in the major map, so aim for the gaps!

A major root position

E altered scale from b4/3rd

Loops

To really develop your ear for hearing and resolving tension, use a looper and record a simple rhythm (nothing too busy right now) using an Amaj7 chord for two to four measures. Practice by playing the E altered map over it and resolve it to the A major map. Listen for the tension and resolution. The E altered map should sound "wrong" and unstable (maybe even awful) over the Amaj7. Learn to hear it and be in tune with it. This is our ear training. Be musical and use phrasing and rhythmic variation freely, then let your ears guide you and your fingers will follow while your brain takes notes. This is an excellent way to learn that will fast-track your ears and fingers to hear and resolve tension like a pro.

Another helpful way to practice your melodic phrasing while hearing these arpeggios in context is to record a simple loop or backing track with an E7 or E7altchord (you can look up altered chords online or in a book or use something like the Hendrix chord; E7#9). An E7 with no 5th is a great voicing to use for this approach (look up shell voices). Now play the altered map and resolve it into the major map. Really get to know how these maps work and sound together because they're just intersecting streets in the same town.

As this becomes more comfortable and you're hearing and revolving lines with increasing fluency, record loops or backing tracks using these variations:

- E7 – Amaj7 (E altered to A major maps)

- Bm7 – E7 (A major to E altered maps; moving into tension)

- Bm7 – E7 – Amaj7 (A major to E altered and back to A major maps; moving from consonance into dissonance and resolving)

- Bm7 – E7 – Amaj7 (E altered over both Bm7 – E7 and resolve to Amaj7)

You can use the A major maps over any of the chords from the A major scale (Amaj7, Bm7, C#m7, Dmaj7, E7, F#m7, and G#m7b5 and any of those chords with their extensions 9, 11, or 13, i.e. F#m9, Bm11, E13, etc.). These can help you hear the sounds you can create playing in this key center.

Let your ears guide you and you'll naturally find the sounds you like, want and need. Remember to play the maps musically, moving in any direction, from anywhere within the map, phasing musically and rhythmically, and letting your ears develop and your fingers adapt as you explore all the sounds and possibilities contained within the maps.

Doing this, you should progress very quickly and become quite adept at moving around all over the place, slipping in and out of the maps and between them until they're all interconnected and you can fluently drive throughout the region. After all, you live here now! It happens surprisingly quickly and it's very easy if you just play, exploring and discovering, letting them unfold before you.

Target Shooting

Now let's look at three examples using the E altered and A major maps together to create some simple melodic lines that demonstrate basic tension and resolution. Notice how I play a little of the A major map, switch right into the E altered, then return to the A major map seamlessly with one long phrase rather than like I'm stringing together licks in a cut and paste fashion. This is the result of my practicing moving around in and between the maps while I was learning and practicing them. I've been exploring them, listening to them, and now I'm just being musical with them. These examples were improvised and transcribed on the spot instead of composed because this method lends itself to instantly creating intelligent, deliberate, melodic lines.

Notice how I'm not just moving around randomly anymore. Now I'm being musical and creating lines. I can't stress this enough: be musical and use phrasing and rhythmic variations as soon as possible. Although we're just playing portions of the maps ascending and descending, don't hesitate to pivot off a note or double back on the shape you just used before moving on, and don't wait to use hammer-ons, pull-offs, and slides to add some legato to your lines. You don't have to pick everything.

IMPORTANT: At first you may find yourself creating nice phrases in the major map and nice phrases in the altered map, which is definitely something you want to become fluent in, but for really great jazz phrasing you also want to create long, flowing phrases that combine both maps without losing a beat, which is why moving from one to another using the nearest available note in either is so important almost from the start. This helps you create nice fluid lines that flow smoothly right over the chord changes. This interplay between the maps is a huge key to jazz phrasing and improvising.

You're always playing through the tension and toward the place of resolution, whether it's the temporary resolution of finished phrases and movement to other grounded chords in the solo section or it's a final resolution to the tonic chord or another chord in the song's key. It could even be to a resolution in some key the song modulates to. Either way, always play toward your points of resolution and you'll learn to anticipate upcoming chords where you resolve the tension.

Chapter Three: More Miles from Our Maps

Out of Order

Now that we've been using our maps for a bit, exploring and creating simple melodic lines using smaller portions of them together, we can begin adding more interest and variety to our lines by playing the notes out of order, switching them up, which makes our lines more intervallic and angular, a common feature of modern playing.

Let's take a look at the first four notes of the A major map.

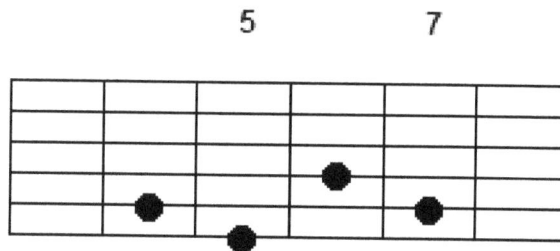

Up until now, we've been using bits and pieces of our maps in ascending and descending fragments, like in Example 1 below, mixing our major and altered maps. Look at the treble staff and notice how the curve of the notes has a nice, smooth contour as they rise and fall.

However, we can also play these notes in any order, creating *permutations*. Using the A map fragment in Example 1, let's take a look at the possibilities for just this set of notes and remember, this can be done with *any* group of notes: three, four, five, etc. This greatly expand our options for creating interesting melodic lines from the major and altered maps. Also, look at the treble staff again and notice how the notes jump around a little more unpredictably and without the smooth contour. They're more jagged, with sharper angles. They're *angular*.

It's alright to play through the examples just to get the idea, but don't turn this into an exercise! This is just a demonstration of the possibilities. You can get bogged down in endless exercises if you try doing this with portions of maps. Instead, just continue creating phrases and lines by using the major and altered maps together to create tension and resolution while keeping this approach in mind and using this idea for new variations. Keep your ears open they'll guide your fingers to the sounds you like.

Let's take a look at some examples I came up with while doing this on the fly. I'm also going to move into other map positions, opening up the neck a little more and doing some traveling along the fretboard, something we want to be doing as soon as possible.

It's Okay to Skip

No, really! It's okay to skip! Just don't run before you can walk. Now that we're exploring the new world of possibilities that come from playing the notes in different orders, the next logical step is to begin skipping notes. That's right, just pull a note out! Ignore it! You can use it later, if you like. It'll still be there. But you don't always have to use it every time.

As with everything here, we can do this with any portion and any group of notes in the major or altered maps. Let's take a look at the first four notes of our root position A major map again and see what we can do with them if we skip notes.

I don't want to show more possibilities because I don't want you practicing these like they're exercises. I did that at first and quickly discarded the idea because it was much quicker just to keep the idea in mind and simply continue being musical and playing while exploring and creating lines with it because there are so many possibilities and grasping the concepts and using them right away is so much more important than getting tied up with endless non-musical exercises.

You can play these on sets of three, four, five, or even all six strings and remember this applies to all maps. So, let's see some examples of this idea in action with our maps.

Example 7 mixes skipping notes in the first measure and *both* skipping notes and playing notes out of order in the second measure.

Example 8 mixes skipping notes *and* playing them out of order in the first measure.

Example 9 is a little more extreme but sounds great and is fun to play.

In Black and White

We're learning how to paint so many colors just using black dots and white dots. Who woulda thunk it? So now seems as good a time as any to expand our palate and use black and white dots *together*. This will take us to the next level and open up so many new routes of travel through our sonic terrain.

If we play black and white notes consecutively, then we can begin adding scalar passages to our map lines. Artfully combining this approach with the previous ideas expands our mobility and modes of expression considerably.

Let's look at the first half of the A major map once again and play that portion of the map ascending with the black dots then descending using all the black and white dots together.

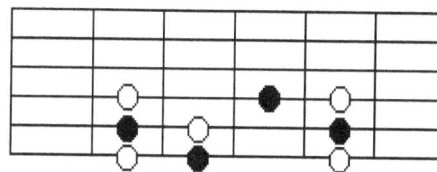

We can add a whole string of consecutive notes anywhere we want *or* we can discriminately add *select* notes wherever we want to color our maps in a variety of ways. We can use *any* selection of black and white dots together in different ways for creating our melodic lines, using both the major and altered maps, playing notes consecutively, out of order, or skipping notes for a whole new world of possibilities.

Let's look at some of these possibilities with our first four black dots alone while adding just one white dot into the mix in each example.

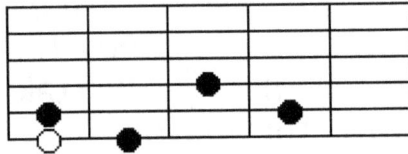

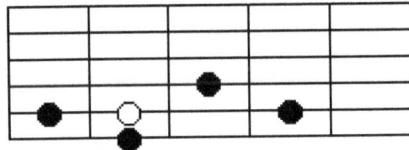
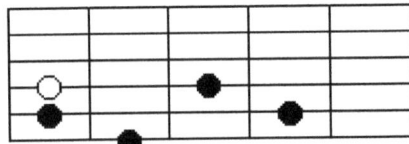
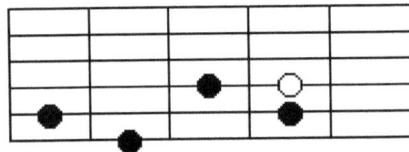

Play through these just to get an idea of what you can do *anywhere* within the major and altered maps and then start exploring and developing your ideas using *all* the new sounds and approaches at your disposal. All we're doing is exploring different ways of dissecting and using our maps to create variety so we can generate more interesting lines with infinite combinations, limited only by our imagination and taste.

As with *all* concepts in this method, you can play notes out of order and skip notes, or do both (try skipping strings for even more wide interval ideas). You can play black and white dots together, selecting whatever you like to get whatever sounds you want. Always remember how the major and altered maps relate and work together, interacting, intertwined in an endless sonic dance that you choreograph.

Now let's look at some examples that I've discovered while exploring this idea. Here's where we'll really start using our guitar techniques, employing slides and legato, even economy and sweep picking or hybrid picking if you want to shred a little. It's okay; this book is not style specific. We're just moving into the realm of jazz phrasing and how to get those great sounds into our own playing at the speed of improvisation.

The dashed bracket shows where I'm using the black and white dots together for scale fragments.

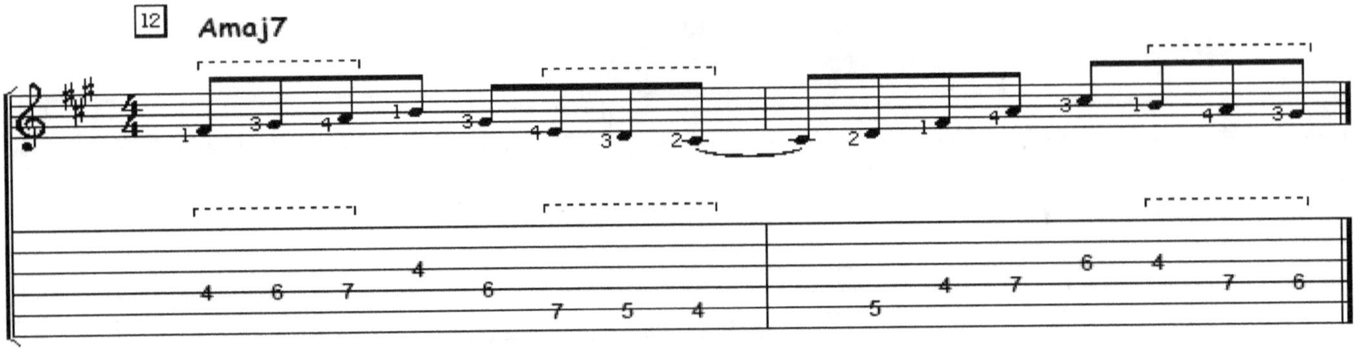
12
Amaj7

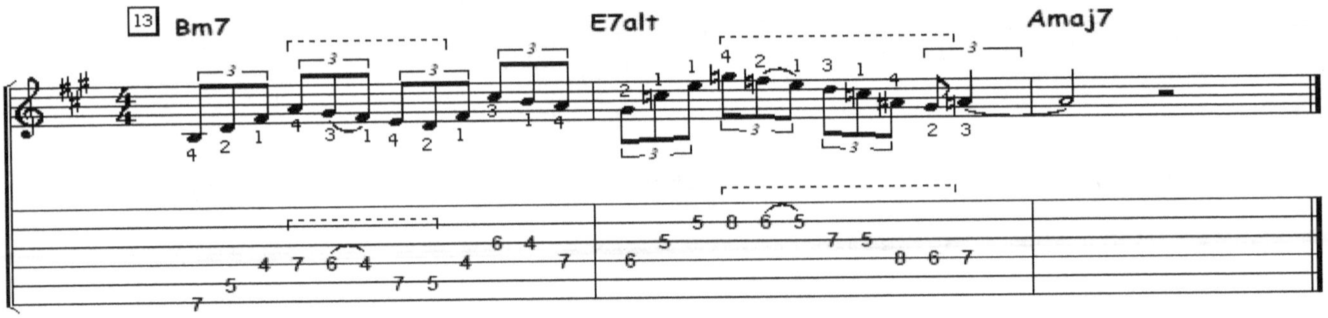
13
Bm7
E7alt
Amaj7

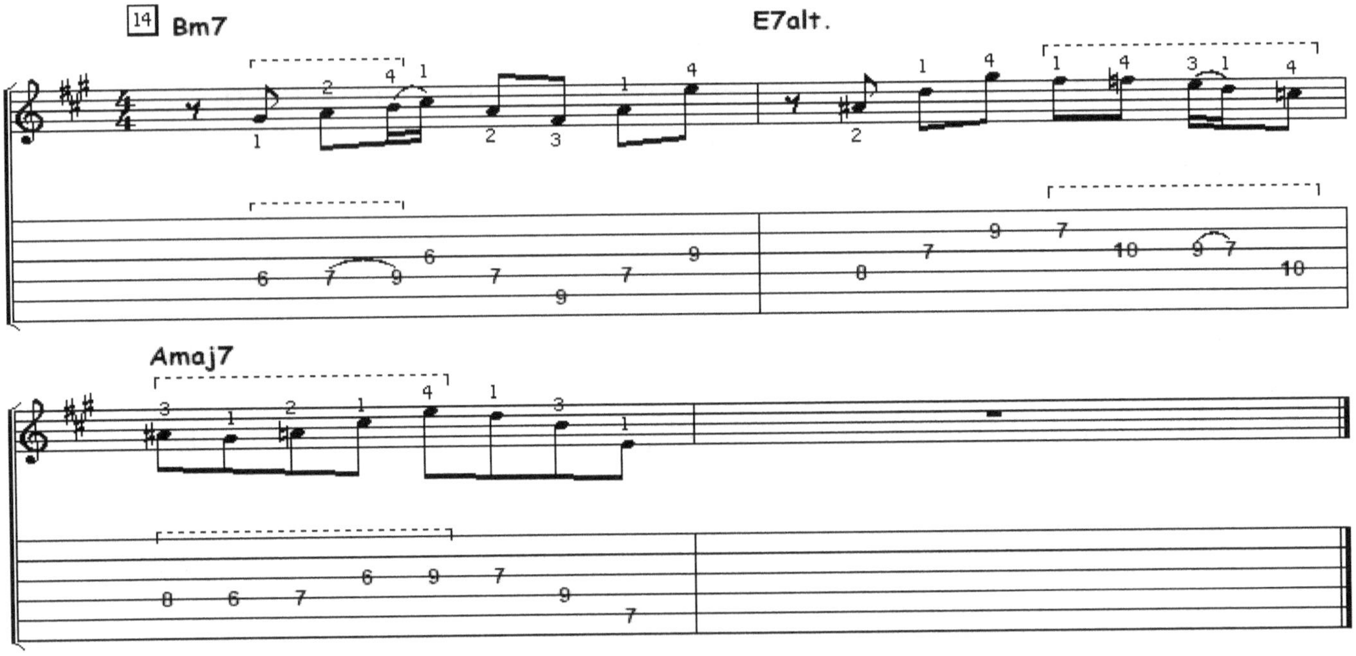
14
Bm7
E7alt.
Amaj7

Smooth Operator

A very valuable and helpful tip for moving smoothly between maps when playing scalar passages is to continue through them stepwise and connect them as if they were a single scale. Trying to jump around intervallically between them can sound much more obvious and, in many cases, jarring. Of course, in time, that might be exactly the effect you want.

Example 15 demonstrates this idea as we move in black and white between the E altered and A major maps. I use the E on the second string, fifth fret as the transition point. This note is shared by both maps. It's the root of E altered and the fifth of A major. The E is circled for easy identification.

Another strategic option is to simply continue to the next available note in the map you're moving to, as demonstrated in Example 16. This creates what I call incidental chromaticism. Again, our transition note is circled.

Notice how we're always building on what we've learned before, using everything together, and the lines are becoming more sophisticated as a result. Once we have the maps as a foundation, we simply use our building blocks to bring them to life by manipulating and embellishing those core maps. And we're not done yet. Have fun!

Chapter Four: Use the Fourths

A cornerstone of the modern jazz sound and style is the use of fourth intervals. A fourth interval is a note that is four diatonic notes above or below the note we are playing, so it's often a note at the same fret on an adjacent string to the one we're playing. The exception is when the note is a b5th interval, also known as a #4th, or when we're playing between notes between the 3rd and 2nd strings.

Fourths give our lines a great hip, modern, angular sound, and sound great when played out of order and when combined with fragments of the maps played out of order or skipping notes. This makes our lines very jagged and intervallic. It's a great area to explore for jazz-rock and fusion playing and works really well in a more modal context where you're playing in one key center for a longer time than in traditional jazz.

Notice how they're right there, lurking inside our maps if we look at them from a slightly new angle. Just play the black dots or the white dots across adjacent frets and you're playing fourths. The following diagram displays the standard major map we've been using and is followed by a couple diagrams that show the fourths as they fall across the frets in sets of white and sets of black.

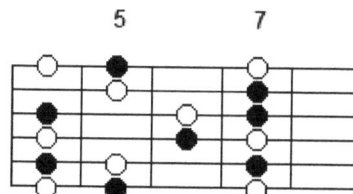

A major root position

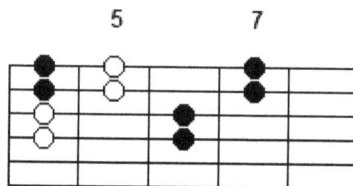

fourths on top 4

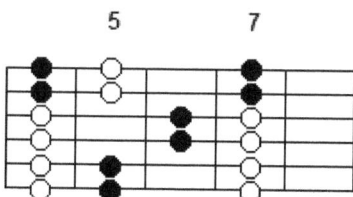

fourths

Fourths are very easy to find and incorporate into your playing, so don't turn looking for and learning them into an exercise, Instead, begin using them right away, slipping them into your lines and combining them with the ideas you've already learned and listening for what you like. In the major map, you'll find one sharped fourth. In the altered map you'll find one sharped fourth and one flatted fourth that will look like a major 3rd. Just use them and play on.

In Example 1, I stagger fourths across the strings in groups of three, a sound I really like.

Example 2 is a more modern approach to playing a line over a ii-V-I progression. It begins with a simple map climb and then launches into a volley of fourths moving through the A major map and E altered map before returning to the A major map to resolve.

We're going to cover *chromaticism* and *side-slipping* very soon, but it won't really encompass the very simple technique used in Example 3, which is nothing more than taking an idea and moving it up or down one fret at a time, starting in key, moving out of key, then ending back in key at a new place on the fretboard. It's a very common technique used in rock, metal, and sometimes blues, but suits modal jazz and fusion quite nicely and sounds really great with fourths.

43

Three Fourths

While we're on the topic of playing with fourths, we can also play combinations of thirds and fourths. You might recognize these as common triad inversions. Simple as these are, notice how they further expand our growing vocabulary as we explore our maps. By the way, for the shredders out there, fourths and "three fourths" are great places to use your economy and sweep picking if you're moving in the modern fusion and progressive direction. Listen to Frank Gambale for inspiration here.

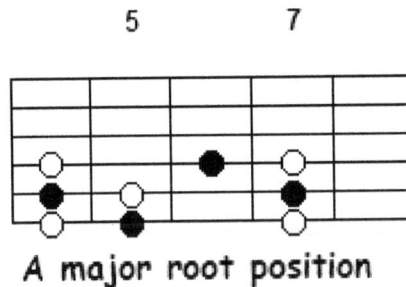

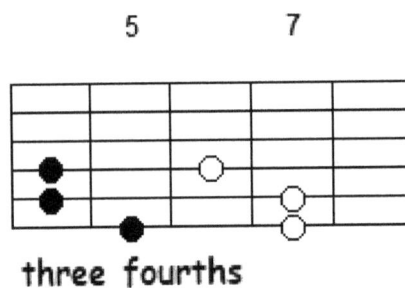

5   7

A major root position

5   7

three fourths

Example 4 shows some of these interval combinations available in the first half of the A major map.

4

Let's play some lines using this idea. The brackets show where I'm using this approach.

Example 6 demonstrates playing some of the intervals out of order. Notice how I move into each one from the next nearest note above or below, although you don't have to do this. Skipping helps create very modern sounding lines.

Example 7 breaks things down into shorter phrases that breathe a little for more rhythmic variation.

Chapter Five: Kind of Blues

The Pentatonics Within

You're really going to like this one because it will propel you ahead by leaps and bounds almost instantly since you're suddenly going to have a place to use all your great blues and rock licks with the maps while also discovering many more new sounds as you combine everything together for a hearty new stew. This is a major bridge between what you're learning and what you already know.

I'm going to start with the pentatonic scale that's lurking within the altered map because there's only one and because it just has all the great fuzzy altered tones that give the altered map its unique sound. This is a favorite of John Scofield and you can get a lot of very hip, modern-sounding bluesy phrasing using this beautiful pentatonic position, combining it with the altered map and all the ideas we've explored so far, resolving it our major map so we can land on our feet and take a bow after we get a little weird and let our freak flag fly.

Be creative here because this helps us play outside with style and grace and pentatonic scales are already familiar territory for most guitarists. As soon as you're comfortable, start incorporating all those blues and rock licks you know and adapting them to the jazz and fusion sound. Try swinging them a little to keep it jazzy too.

Here are our pentatonic scales within the altered map.

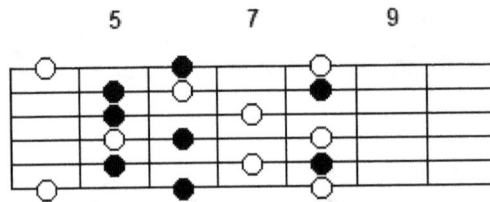

E altered from b4/3rd

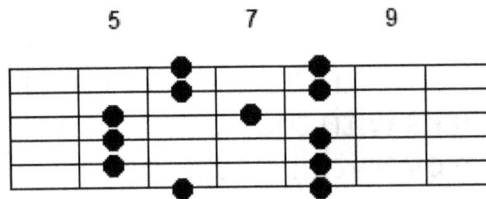

E altered pentatonic

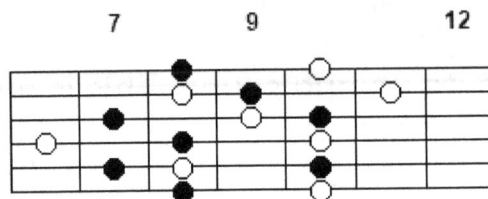

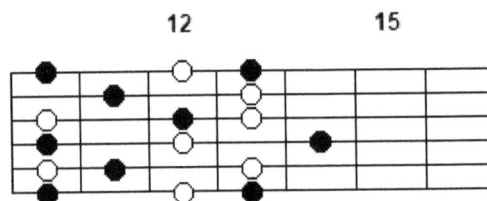

E altered from b6/b13 (#5)

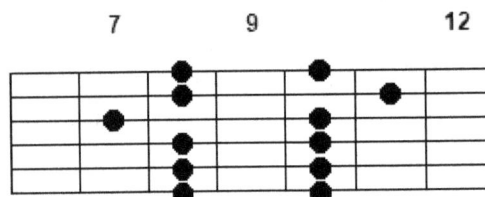

E altered pentatonic

E altered from b7th

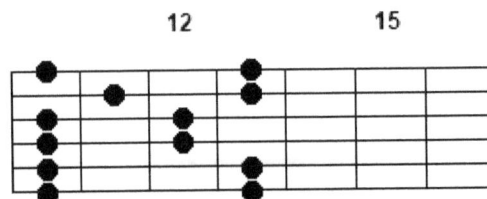

E altered pentatonic

48

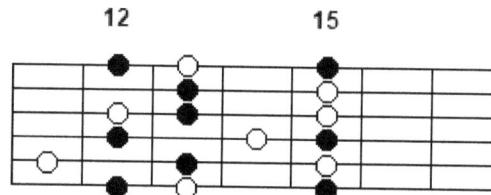

E altered from root

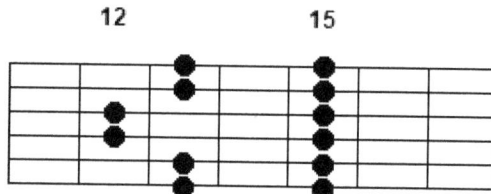

E altered pentatonic

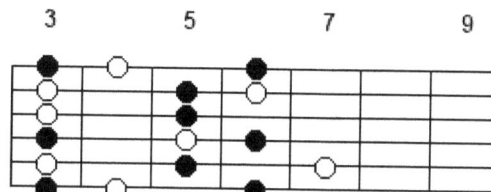

E altered from b3/#9

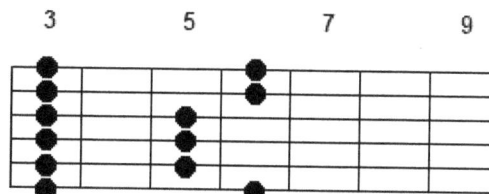

E altered pentatonic

An easy way to learn this is to just begin inserting pentatonic phrases with portions of the E altered map and all the techniques we've explored up to this point while always remembering to resolve our altered ideas into the major map just above or below the position we're in. Sneak it in there and keep in mind that we're resolving the E altered map to the A major map, usually using chromatic resolution to the nearest note as our smooth move, although you can explore and develop your ideas however you like as you move forward. This is your journey and I'm just the Sherpa, guiding you as you're starting out (tips are accepted).

Here are some examples of using our E altered pentatonic map resolving to the A major map.

That should be enough to get you going.

Now we're *really* going to take this idea to the next level and look at the A major map. Within the major map there are *three* pentatonic scales and there are no rules forbidding us from using them *all*, so you can go crazy with those pentatonic licks and ideas you've been sitting on so patiently up until this point. You can mix and match them in your phrasing like we do everything else. Let's take a look at what we have at our disposal.

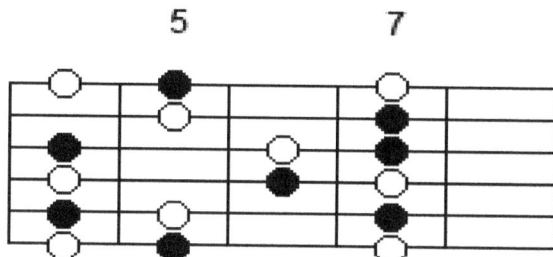

A major from root

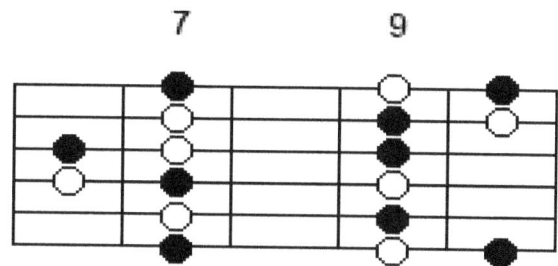

A major from 2nd

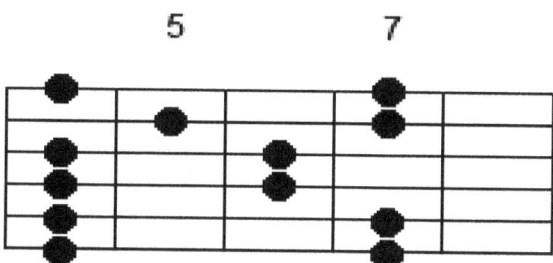

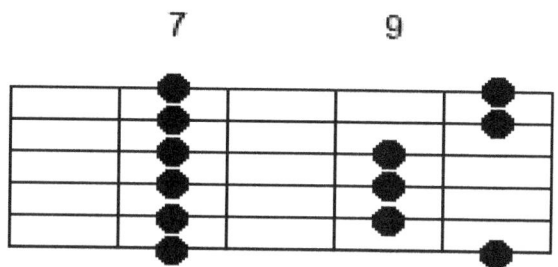

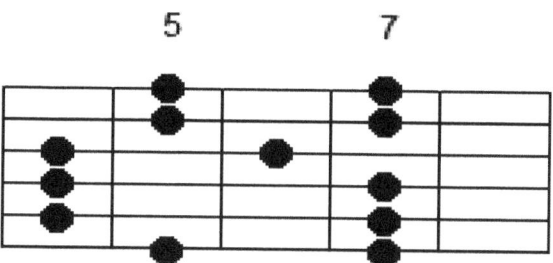

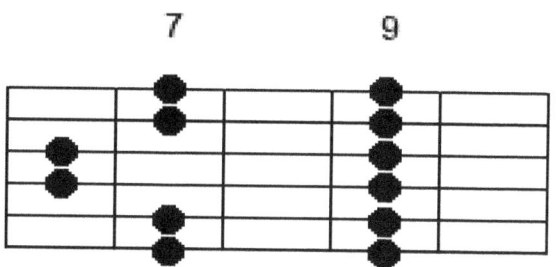

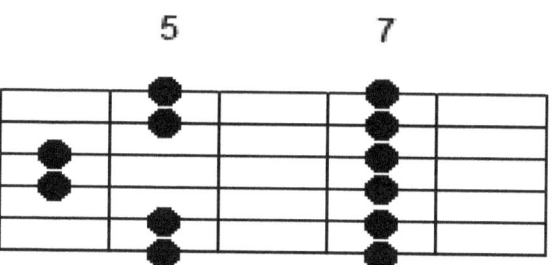

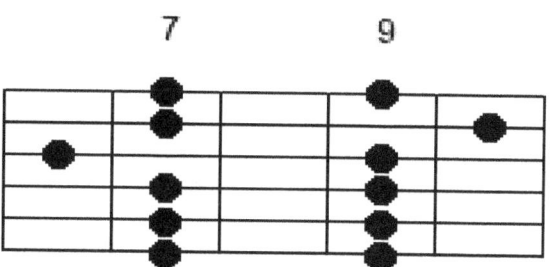

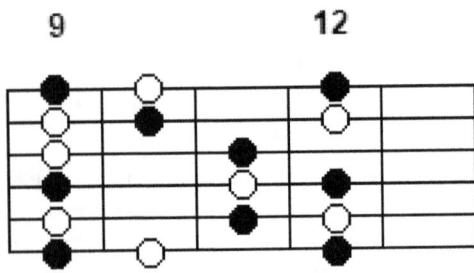

A major from 3rd

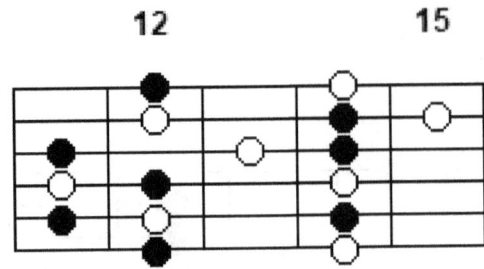

A major from 5th

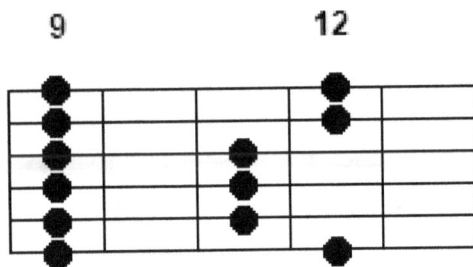

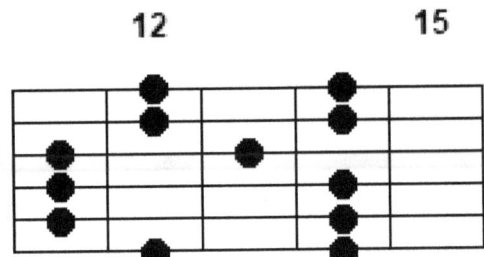

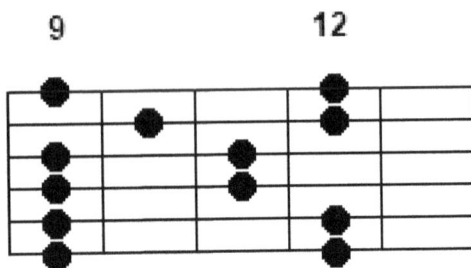

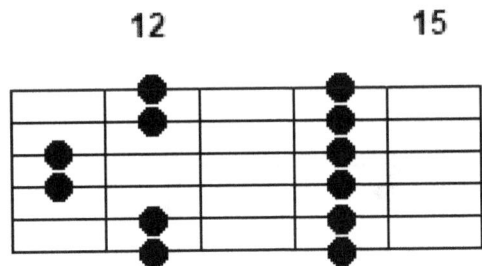

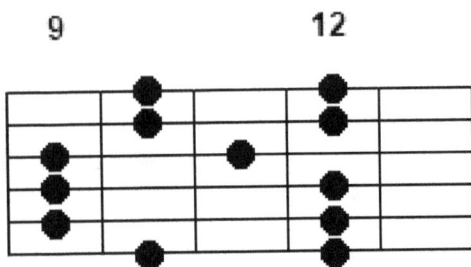

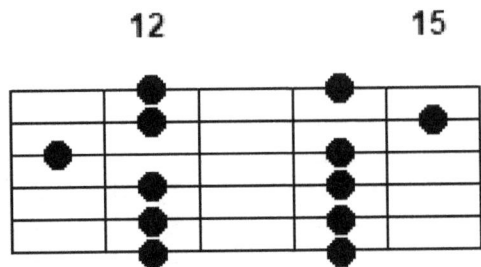

52

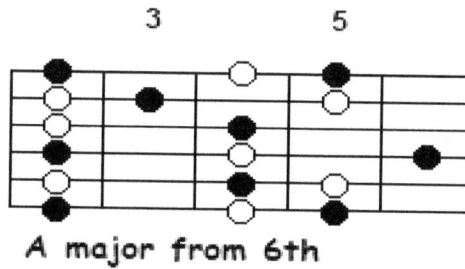

A major from 6th

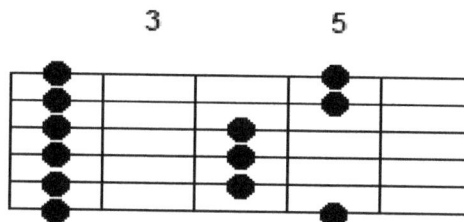

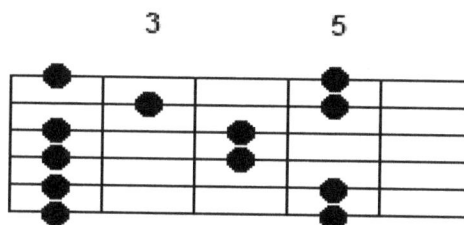

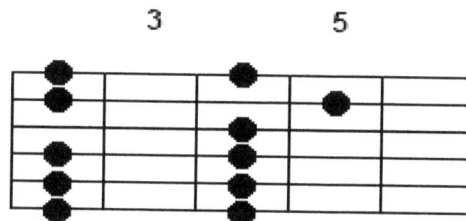

Now you should be getting some real bang for your buck as you use the major *and* altered maps together with all the ideas we've discussed so far *plus* using those old familiar pentatonic scales and licks we've all learned so early on in our playing. Those blues, rock, and blues-rock licks can all find a place as we mix them with our maps and almost instantly expand our vocabulary by leaps and bounds. Just remember to swing and groove like a jazz cat and you'll be in the zone.

Let's start using the pentatonics lurking within the major map and create some new jazzy lines with a twist of blues (or a twisted blues).

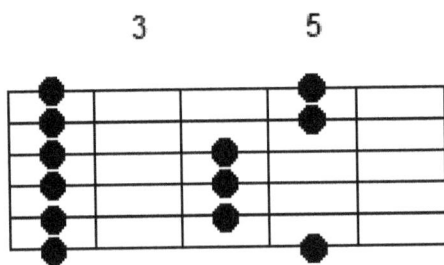

Something Special

If you haven't already noticed, the major map shares a pentatonic scale shape identical to the pentatonic for the altered map it's paired with. In fact, the two pentatonic positions are only a *half* step apart! This gives us access to some creative melodic bluesy mayhem (or not so bluesy, if you wanna get weird!).

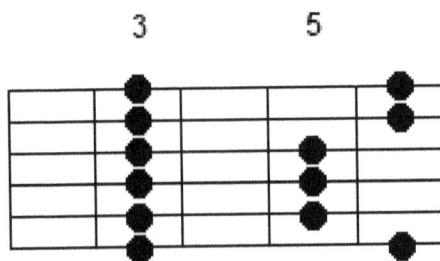

Personally, I don't tend to go for very traditional sounds when I move into this territory, but that's just me. I love the modern, angular sounds that jump around a little more. Here we go.

This should jumpstart you for your own exploration because this is really about learning the MAS4JI method and discovering your own voice using it as a guide.

Chapter Six: Chromaddict

Filling in the Gaps

It's my sincere hope that MAS4JI is transforming your playing and perspective considerably as you discover new ways to apply old information by looking at it from some slightly different angles. I say that because now we're really going to bust the floodgates wide open and get things *really* flowing with *chromatic* notes, an instrumental backbone of the jazz sound throughout pretty much all eras. This chapter will propel your playing into the stratosphere as we take the A train straight into the heart of the jazz terrain. Prepare to become addicted to the chromatic.

Chromatic notes are simply notes are not in the key you're playing in, hence they are not *diatonic* to the key. They are the notes in between the notes you're playing in your maps. They are the notes that fill the gaps in your maps.

Essentially, we're already using chromaticism as we weave back and forth between the A major and E altered maps. But that doesn't mean we can't kick things up a notch or ten. Also, with chromaticism, we can add *more* dissonance to our lines even while we're resolving them, or when we're lingering on a chord vamp for a bit and we want to tweak our lines a little and add some spice.

There are three main ways we're going to use chromatic notes with our maps: approach tones, passing tones, and enclosures. Let's look at each one and then use them with our maps.

Approach Tones

An approach tone is a note that's not in the key and that precedes a note that is in key from a half step above or below. Here are a couple simple examples using our root position A major map. The approach tones are circled. Notice how *jazzy* our maps sound without even using the altered map!

It's that simple!

Passing Tones

This is not the same thing as passing wind, which is what you do in a woodwind section and you'll hear more in classical music (I do like classical music!). Passing tones are out-of-key chromatic notes that you play *in between* the notes you meant to play. Okay, they're chromatic notes you play between the diatonic ones… with purpose. They add really nice spice to your lines without giving your listeners heartburn.

The following examples target the A root of the A major map, so these examples would work great over an Amaj7, but you can use passing tones anywhere . . . and everywhere if you want to go crazy (or drive band mates crazy).

In Examples 3 and 4 the passing tones should be pretty obvious (hint: three notes in a row). Examples 5 and 6 are something I like to do by playing the passing tone then faking the listener out and playing another diatonic note before going to the note I'm aiming for. It works really great with the minor third interval here but experiment with other intervals too. The passing tones are the notes I hammer on or pull off to and all passing tones are marked with a plus (+) sign for easy identification.

Examples 7 and 8 use passing tones in longer lines.

Chromatic Enclosures

Chromatic enclosures use a mix of diatonic and chromatic notes to circle a tone like sharks in a cartoon before hitting it instead of going right in for a bite. To keep things simple I'm going to demonstrate two very common chromatic enclosures here. You can add more notes at your own discretion. Examples 9 and 10 will enclose the 3rd (C#) of the Amaj7 chord from the root position A major map. It's not uncommon to target a note using two strings, which requires a little stretch. Examples 11 and 12 target the root, but you can target *any* notes in the map you like.

Some enclosures have less notes, some more, and some hit the targeted note and continue with the enclosure before returning to land on it. The following examples include some variations.

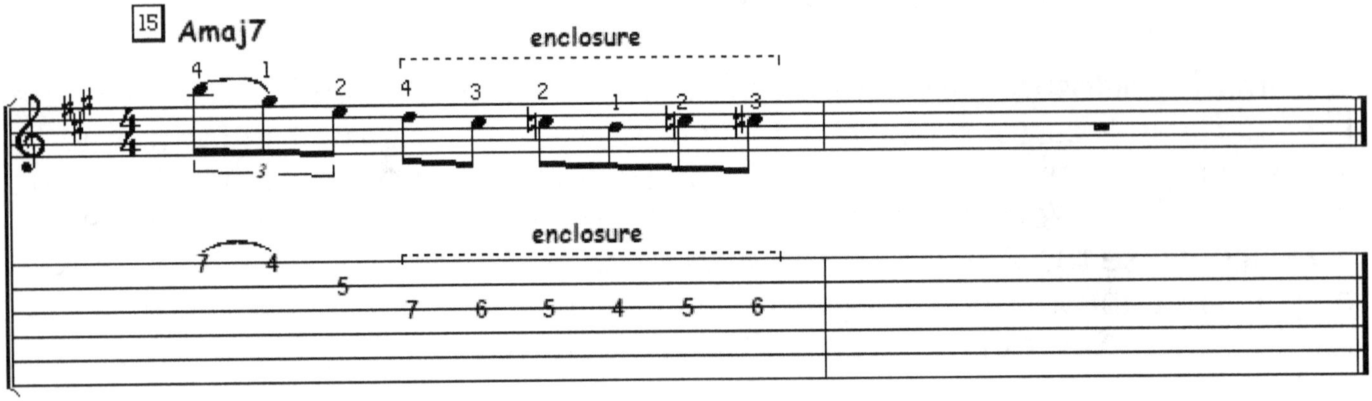
15
Amaj7
enclosure
enclosure

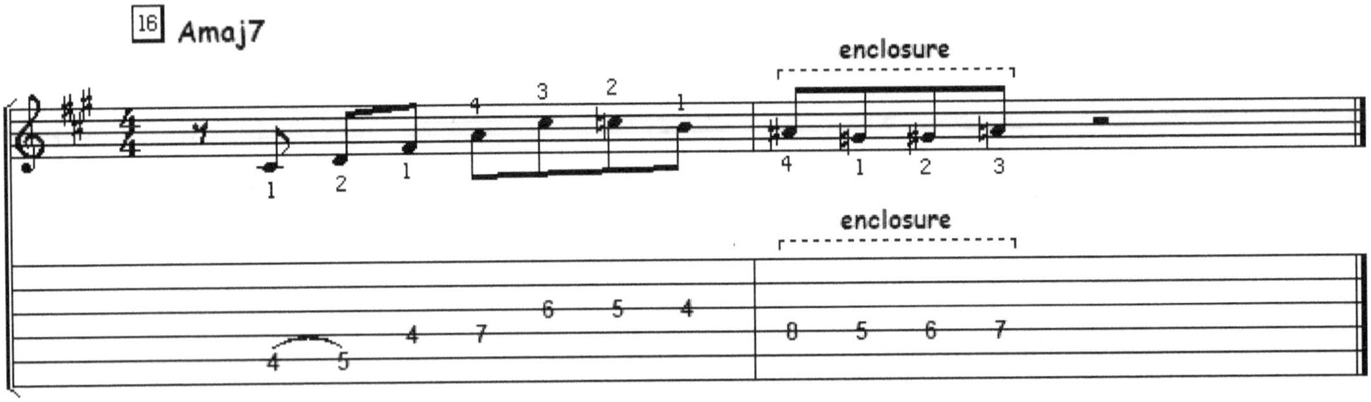
16
Amaj7
enclosure
enclosure

Now let's use our chromatic notes and create some nice lines. The chromatic notes are circled. In Example 17, the first measure features a passing tone and the second measure has an approach tone. Notice how they really jazz up a simple line that's otherwise right in key over the tonic chord.

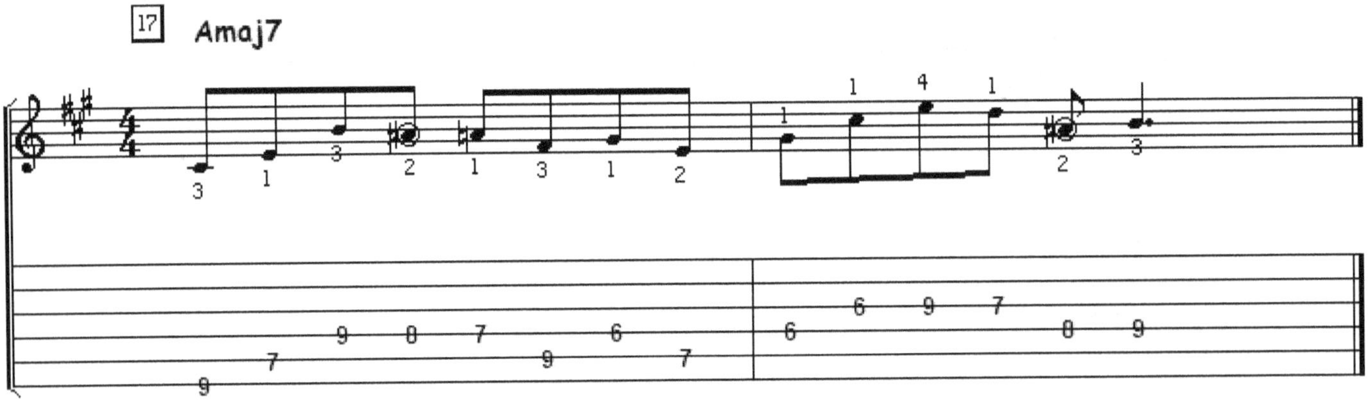
17
Amaj7

Try your ideas with different rhythms. These fit nicely over the Amaj7. The chromatic notes are circled here.

In Example 21, the chromatic tones are marked with a plus (+) sign.

Chapter Seven:
Slip Sliding Away
(Side-Steppin')

Side-slipping (or *side-stepping*) is an incredibly cool technique that, like most here, expands your vocabulary immensely, and you don't even have to learn anything new. It's an especially handy tool for playing over static chords in modal tunes or anyplace where a chord is played for two or more measures or a bass note is droned. It's a way of adding interest and momentum to lines that could otherwise sound a little stale or boring because there's not much harmonic motion. It's also a great device to mine for all kinds of new ideas and to get a lot of mileage from existing ideas with a little playful experimentation.

You can apply side-slipping to any technique we've been using with the maps. The very simple concept is that, while you're playing a line, you can slip up or down a half step and continue your idea out of key, then pull it back into the key to finish your idea and resolve it. It gives your lines a nice little twist and makes them less predictable. It's surprisingly easy: just shift what you're playing around a little. It's really just another form of chromatic playing that briefly alludes to other sounds outside the key to create melodic tension.

Let's step aside now and take a look at some side-slipping ideas.

Examples 1 and 3 are lines that use side-slipping, both up and down a half step, while Examples 2 and 4 each demonstrate the previous line played without side-slipping so you can see and hear the difference.

Notice how the lines that use side-slipping are a little more colorful and interesting, while the straight-up diatonic lines are a little blander and don't pack quite the same punch. The rest of the samples will feature side-slipping and I'll mark where it is and you can examine them to see where I'm drawing my ideas from within the maps, just offset by a half step up or down.

5 Bm7 or Amaj7

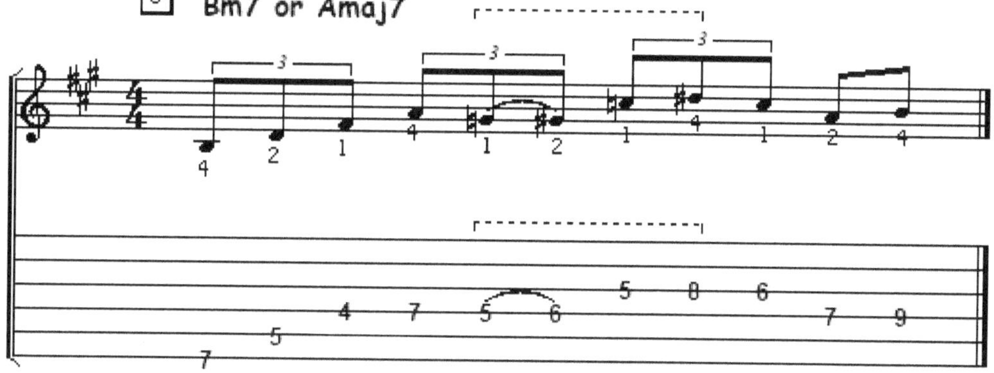

6 Amaj7

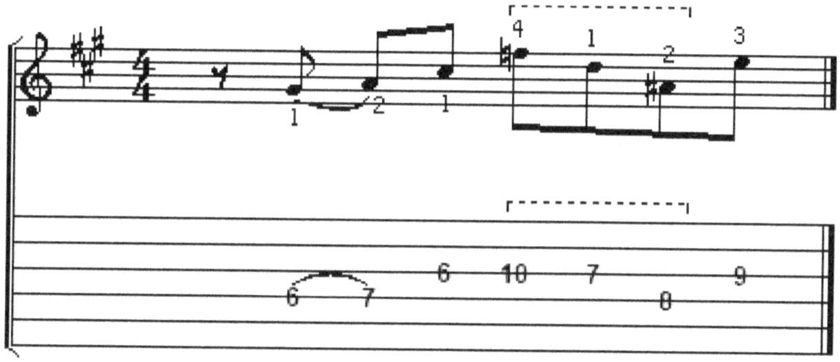

7 Amaj7

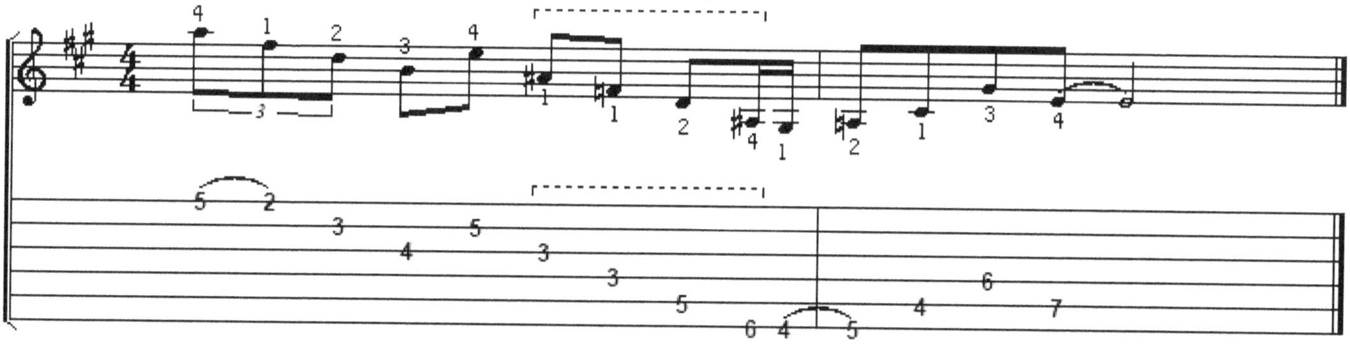

8 Amaj7

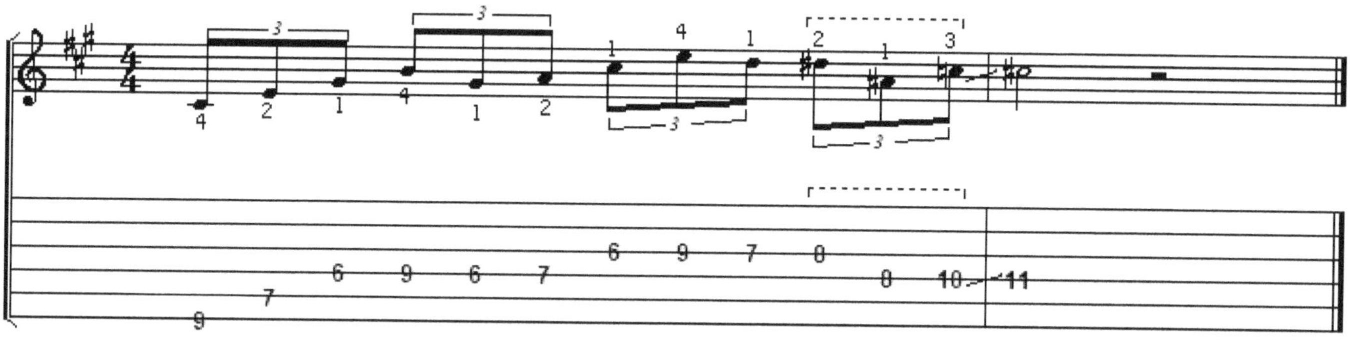

Use this approach with the techniques discussed so far and you'll be playing well within the realm of modern modal jazz-rock fusion. Just follow your ears; they always hears.

That's basically it! That's the heart of improvising jazz lines without a lot of tedious exercises and overthinking techniques with a lot of labels and rules. These guidelines get you to the same destination in less time with less work so you can **play more and think less**. These techniques are melodic and can be mixed and matched pretty freely as long as you keep in mind how to move between the points of tension and resolution. Major is always home and while you may go out for a little bit, you always want to go home at the end. We will use these same simple concepts with anything else we cover from here on out.

Before moving forward, let's review the basic steps to the method:

- **Step 1:** learn the master arpeggios and be able to play them frontward, backward, inside and out, beginning and ending at any point within the pattern, switching between groups of white dots and black dots.

- **Step 2:** Be able to move between the major and altered master arpeggios, playing through them frontward, backward, inside and out, beginning and ending at any point within the patterns, switching between groups of white dots and black dots.

- **Step 3:** Create lines and phrases using fragments of the patterns, switching between the two to create tension and resolution.

- **Step 4:** Create lines and phrases by playing fragments of the master arpeggios *out of order* for more variety and new sounds.

- **Step 5:** Create lines and phrases by playing fragments of the master arpeggios while *skipping* notes.

- **Step 6:** Create lines and phrases using fragments of the master arpeggios and playing black and white dots *consecutively* for scalar sounds.

- **Step 7:** Create lines and phrases using *fourths* intervals from the master arpeggios.

- **Step 8:** Create lines and phrases using combinations of *third and fourth*

- intervals from the master arpeggios.

- **Step 10:** Create lines and phrases by adding *chromatic* approach tones, passing tones, and enclosures.

- **Bonus step:** Create lines and phrases using *side-slipping* on chords that last for one measure or longer.

Chapter Eight:
The Tri-tone Substitute
Teacher

As you learn to play some jazz tunes, you'll inevitably come across something called a *tri-tone substitute*. Very simply, it's just a dominant chord that's a half step above the I chord of the key. More precisely, it's a substitute dominant chord that's a flat 5th away from the V7 chord it's replacing, so it's still a dominant chord resolving to the key. In A major, the ii-V-I (Bm7 – E7 – Amaj7) is substituted with a ii-bII-I (Bm7 – Bb7 – Amaj7). It's really that simple and playing over it is just as simple.

Essentially, you have two choices of what to play over this chord. First, you can simply play the E7 altered map you've been using. Some educated jazz cats will name another scale, but it's just the same notes, different name; don't worry about it. All your altered ideas can be played when you see this progression.

For another color to add to your playing (WARNING: a hint of theory ahead!), Bb7 is the V of Eb major, so you can play the Eb major map over the Bb7 tri-tone sub. It's the major map a flat fifth above (or below) the root major map we're resolving to (Ex: Eb major map to A major map). We'll just keep it at that and you can learn more when you study harmony, which is where academic direction in jazz is very useful, whether from a school, a good teacher, book, or online.

For extra fun, pair up the Eb major and E altered maps and blend them together as a great way of mixing things up and throwing more curveballs at your listener. It'll work as long as you resolve your tension to the A major map when that chord comes up.

On the next page are the A major maps and their Eb major counterparts. Like everything else, use all the tools we have at our disposal to manipulate and embellish the Eb major map as well.

...ajor from root

A major from 2nd

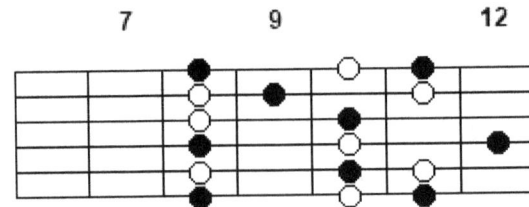

Eb major from 6th

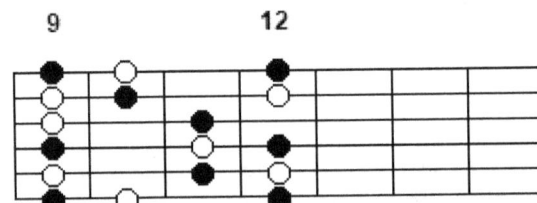

A major from 3rd

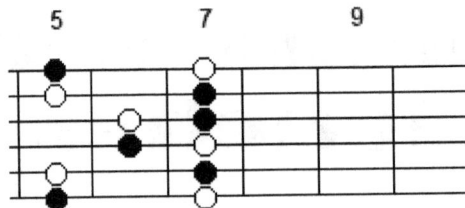

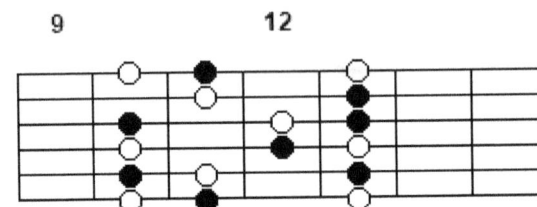

Eb major from root

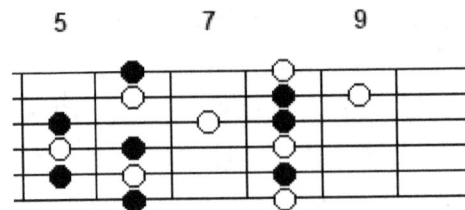

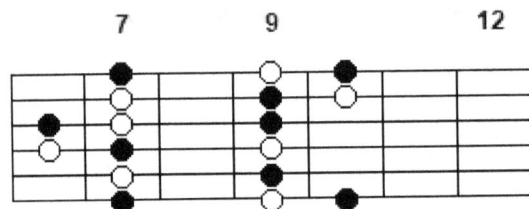

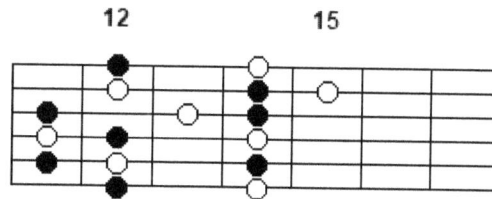
A major from 5th

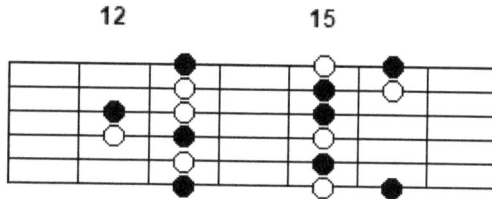
Eb major from 2nd

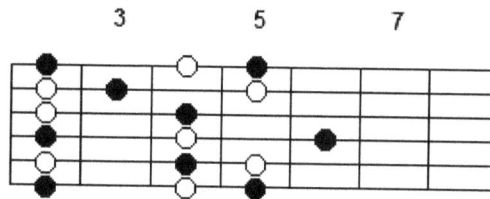
A major from 6th

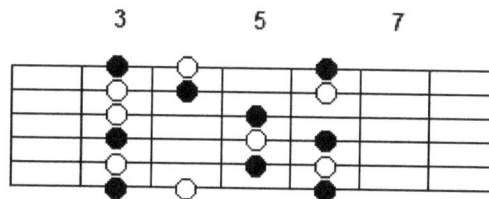
Eb major 3rd

Following are a couple lines that demonstrate this sound.

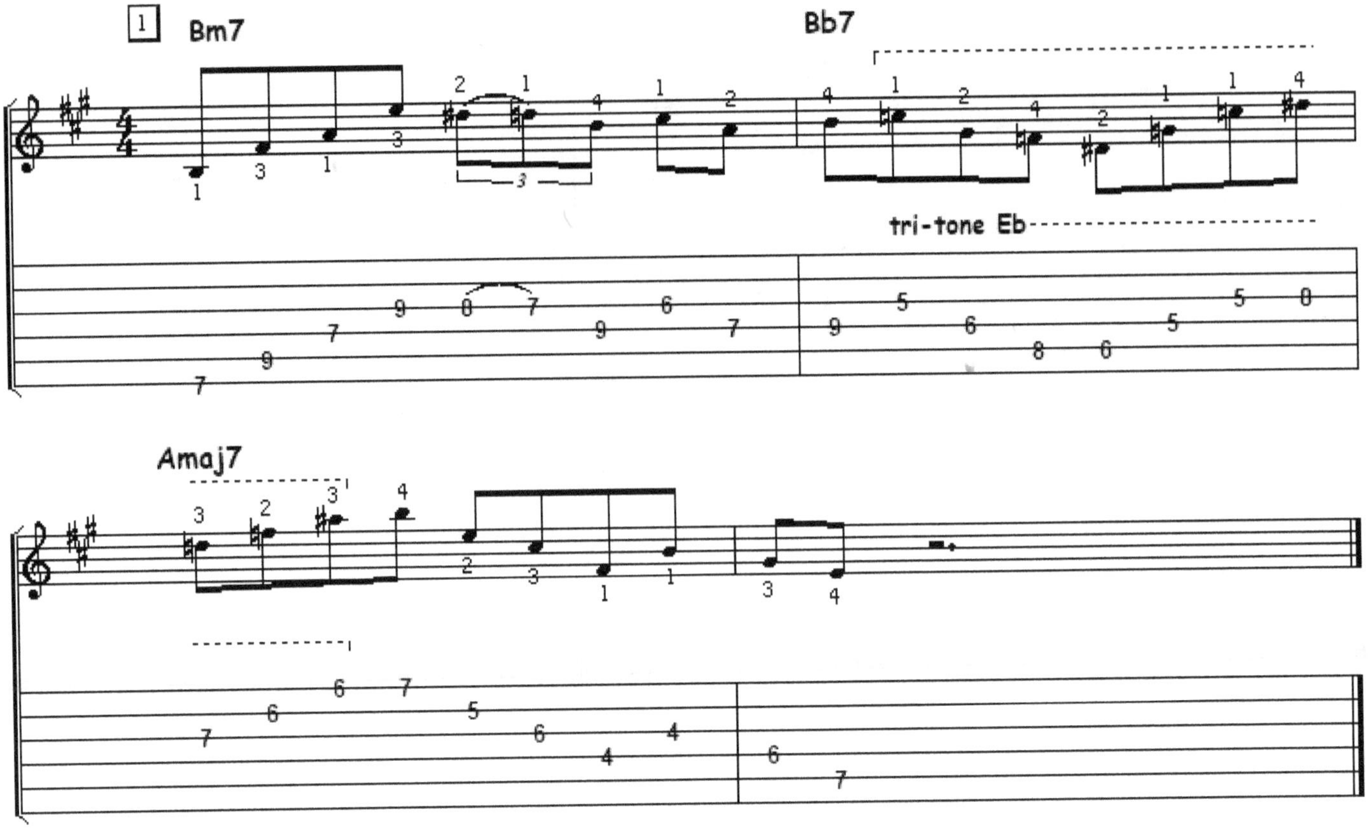
1
Bm7
Bb7
tri-tone Eb
Amaj7

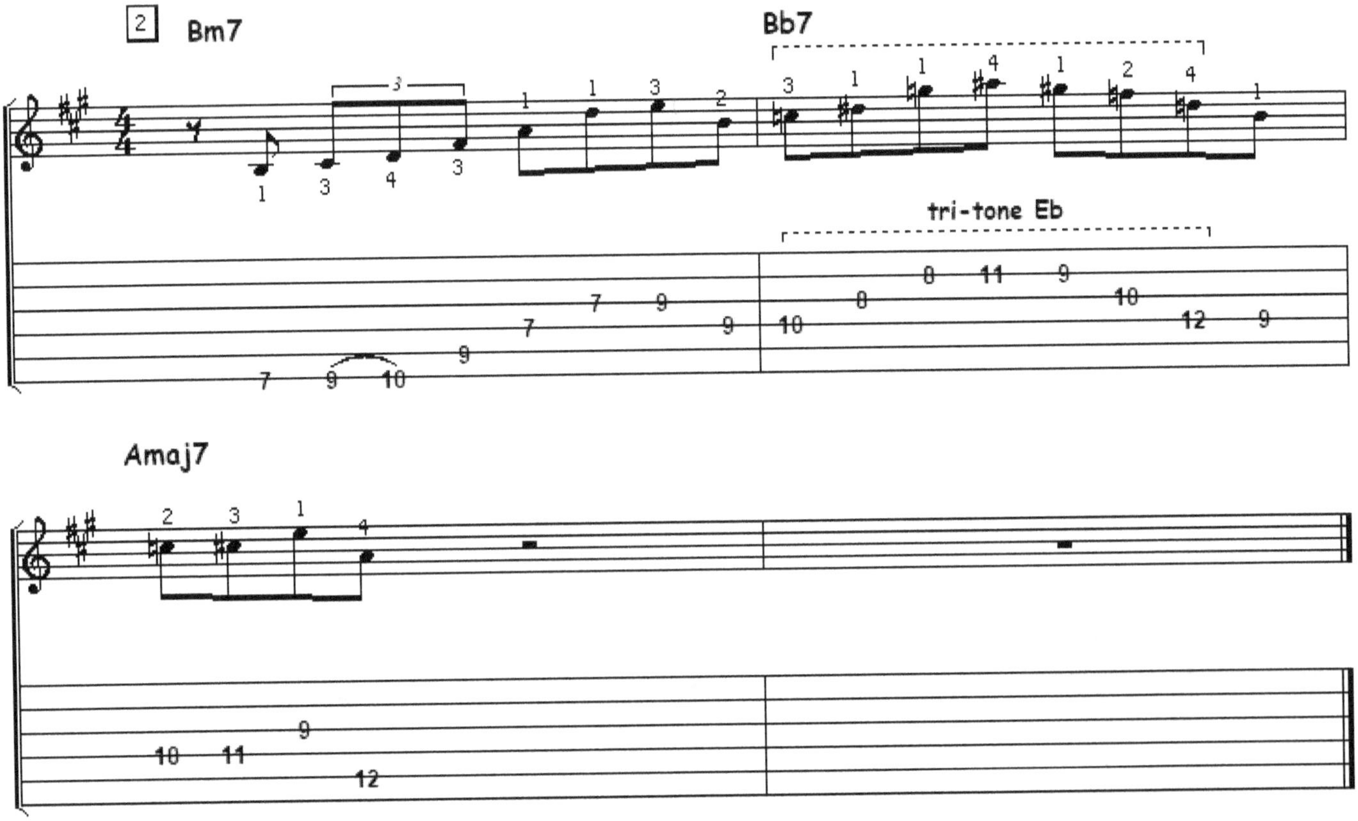
2
Bm7
Bb7
tri-tone Eb
Amaj7

The Tri-Tone Slip

When you find yourself playing over a one-chord vamp or droning riff for a bit, a handy tool to add to your box (so you can play outside the box) is the tri-tone substitution. It's another great way to color outside the lines and still sound great when you're painting with sound.

Imagine you're playing over an Amaj7 vamp for a few measures and you want to add some more zest to your lines, you can slip in and out of the tri-tone map to create a little tension. It's very similar—almost a variation—on side-slipping. Like, side-slipping, this is a very common device used by the modern shred rock-fusion guitarists and one you'll hear all the time once you recognize the sound.

An easy way to orient yourself while improvising lines on the fly is to notice that the map for the tri-tone sub is the map for the major, but played a tri-tone away. So the shapes are very similar in that you're playing the same shape but up one string and up one fret or, conversely, down one string and fret. To demonstrate this, let's look at a portion of each map moving through positions starting in the A major map at the fifth fret, moving to Eb major, then up into A major again. Look at that pattern!

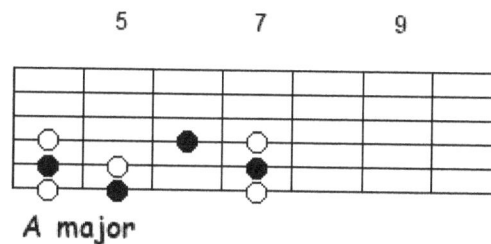

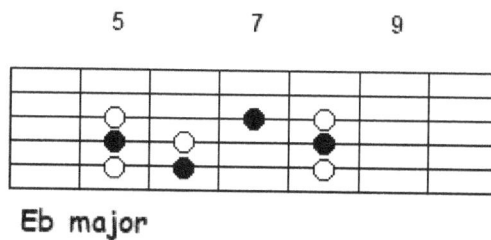

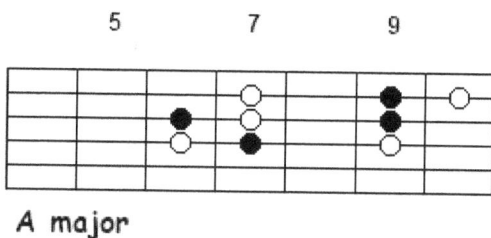

A major

Eb major

A major

Do you see the possibilities? Let's take a look at a couple of simple examples to see how this feels when we play a generic line to orient us with this idea. Example 3 uses more direct fragments of the A and Eb maps. Notice the nice chromaticism in the line. Example 4 moves through fourths with a nice accent on the flatted 5th intervals (try playing a similar line skipping notes; very contemporary). Brackets indicate the tri-tone sub.

Now, let's take a look at this idea in the context of a couple more musical lines.

Example 6 is one for the shredders. This line is very scalar (playing in black and white) and I'm mixing things up a little for a more interesting sound. I'm moving a little motif (pattern) around. The first set of brackets shows where I use the tri-tone slip. The second set of brackets shows where I'm side-slipping using a fragment of one of the pentatonics within the A map along with a chromatic passing tone. I land back in key right on the very last note. This is a good example of a very modern line mixing different approaches we've been learning.

6 Amaj7

Freely: "float" over the rhythm

I really like Example 7. This one also features a scalar motivic idea descending through two positions with a tri-tone slip between the two. It has a slightly more traditional sound that's still pretty hip. Don't forget to swing those eighths!

7 Amaj7

Chromaticism, side-slipping, and the tri-tone slip are not only excellent jazz tools, they're also formidable weapons to have in any rock, metal, progressive, or jam band guitarist's arsenal. The possibilities are limitless with these awesome techniques.

Chapter Nine: Woodshredding

Things get a little more complex here because we're going to dig a little deeper and examine some of the short chord progressions we encounter in jazz standards. Harmony is an area of study that's definitely worth delving into if you want to explore music theory. I'll keep things as basic as I can and we'll focus primarily on the chords and what we want to use with them so we can just play without too much thinking.

I don't like to use the word "exercises," so we'll avoid that one. There are, however, some ways that you'll want to practice the master arpeggios so you'll be ready for some of the most common chord moves you'll inevitably come across. These are more to orient you—to calibrate your fretboard GPS—so you can navigate these twists and turns with comfort and ease. These are some things you definitely want to woodshed if you would shred with some more complex lines.

Cycling

At some point or another you'll come upon a *cycle* progression. There are two that we'll discuss here. The first contains consecutive dominant chords moving in fourths, which are used to create additional tension and delay resolution. In A major you might encounter a cycle that looks something like this: F#7-B7-E7-Amaj7.

This can be daunting for a guitarist that's new to jazz, but we have our maps so we won't get lost. We can play over this progression using the F# altered map over the F#7, B altered map over the B7, E altered map over the E7, and finally resolve with the A major map. This approach will give us great hip, modern sounds over these changes.

The way we can prepare for this kind of movement is to practice the altered maps through fourths. Below are diagrams that demonstrate this in one position, starting with the B altered map: B-E-A-D-G-C. Familiarize yourself with where the root is and which map position you'll use. In the example below, the roots move across the seventh fret, then the eighth on the top two strings. The maps continue on the eighth fret on the bottom four strings (and would be C-F-Bb-Eb-Ab-Db).

Once you do this and continue through the positions you'll see patterns emerging. Those relationships are always the same, so it'll help you never get lost as you begin to move up and down the neck through positions. Your neighboring maps will always be nearby, just like the altered and major maps. In fact, each altered map still has the same relationship to its major map so you know where to resolve when you need to.

This orientation will prepare you for progressions that cycle through dominant chords and jazz blues where you encounter a I-IV-I as dominant chords (I7-IV7-I7). Also, don't forget your cool pentatonics within that feature all the hip, colorful altered tones.

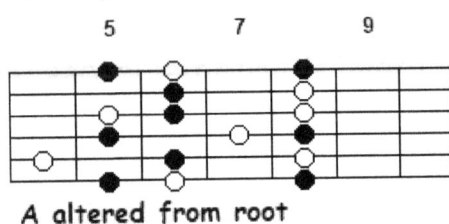

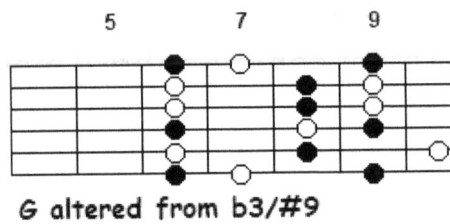

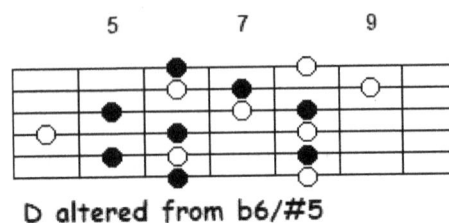

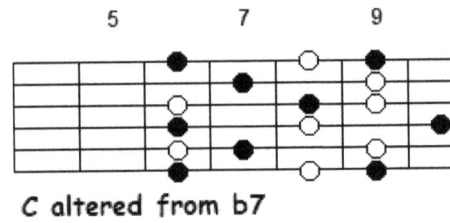

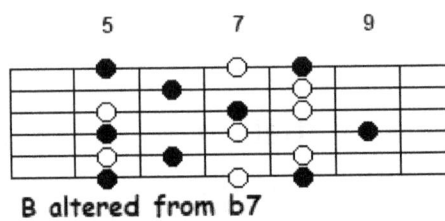

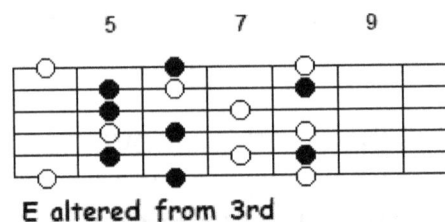

A altered from root

G altered from b3/#9

D altered from b6/#5

C altered from b7

B altered from b7

E altered from 3rd

Cycle Trick

Sometimes those substitute dominant chords fly by at a pretty good clip, even at one for every two beats, so we definitely don't want to spend too much time thinking when we should be playing. The great thing about moving through these scales in fourths is that the note patterns repeat themselves across the strings in any given position on the fretboard, so you can blow over those changes while sticking to easier two or three string sets and playing in a more motivic way, taking a rhythmic or melodic idea and moving it along until you can resolve it. Let's take a look at one of those patterns from the altered maps we just featured above.

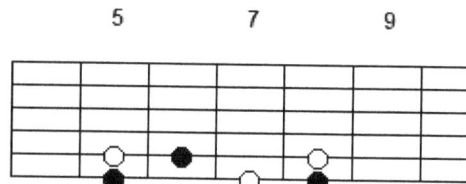

B altered from b7

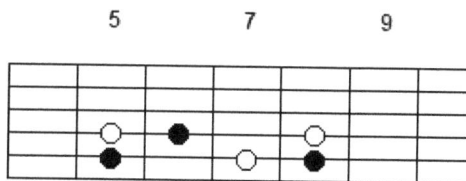

E altered from 3rd

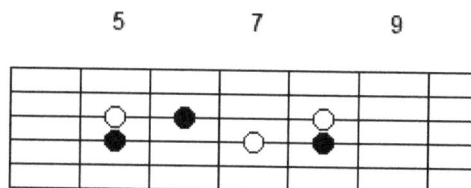

A altered from root

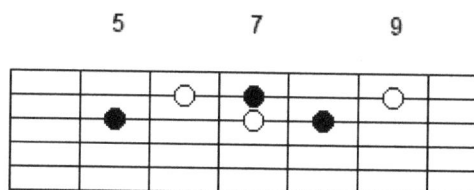

D altered from b6/#5

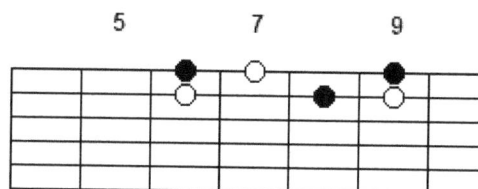

G altered from b3/#9

When you encounter that fast-moving harmony, like B7-E7-A7-G7-C7, for example, you can simply stick to a two or three string portion of the map—like a cell— and develop your ideas in that movable cell until things open up. This way, we can continue to play now and think later. Let's take a look at this in action.

Example 1 demonstrates using a pattern when the chords are just flying by at two per measure and how we play *toward* the point of resolution. Notice how I finish off with a nice jazzier phrase with the G major map once I get to the Gmaj7 chord, where the line resolves. While the fast pattern is fun, easy, and maybe cool, it's the G major line that takes it somewhere and pulls it all together.

Patterns were commonly used by John Coltrane with his *sheets of sound* approach and they're a great device to use when tackling fast-moving progressions . . . or *Coltrane changes*. This also helps us make the connection between the master arpeggios and the scales they contain (not the opposite way, as we're usually taught; arpeggios are more melodic and a better foundation to build on) and scalar patterns are fun when we want to do a little shredding.

Example 2 develops this pattern into a decidedly more interesting, musical, and useful line by fragmenting it and creating phrases swinging the notes and playing them out of order so it doesn't sound like an exercise or a boring run and it keeps our lines from sounding too "black and white."

Another thing to keep in mind is, when confronted with playing over a long one-chord vamp, we can play like this to imply these changes and create additional tension in our lines to keep things interesting. Lines like this are strong *because* they're very rhythmic and melodic patterns and we take them somewhere at the end so that they make sense in the end.

You might also encounter a progression of substitute ii-V chords, like Bm7-E7-Am7-D7-Gmaj7. One great way you can tackle this progression is to blow over each pair of ii-V's with the altered map. For the above progression, you could use the E altered map over the Bm7 and E7, the D altered map over the Am7 and D7, and resolve with the G major map.

An Alternate to the Altered

There's another approach you can use for a more traditional and "safer" sound, and that's to use the major map for the dominant chords, especially if they're not altered in the song and the altered is too *abstract* for the situation (i.e. so you don't lose the gig or get called back for another). This gives you the *Mixolydian* sound. The simple trick is to play the major map that's a *fourth* above or below (whichever's easier to think of) the dominant chord you're playing over.

For the Mixolydian sound with the major maps below you would play them over the chord a *fifth* away (we're just thinking of the V of the key), so we'd play the B major map for F#7. The rest of the positions above would be: E major map for B7, A major map for E7, D major map for A7, G major map for D7, and C major map for G7. You can relate them whichever way is easier for you. I tend to think of the dominant chord I'm working with, say F#7, and associate it with B major. It's a fourth above, so that's next string up on the same fret.

Starting with B major, here are the major maps in one position across the neck:
B-E-A-D-G-C.

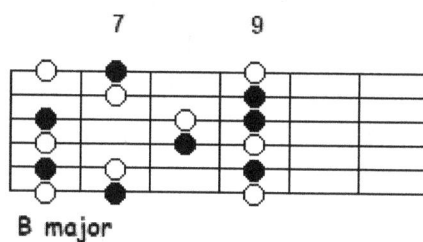

B major

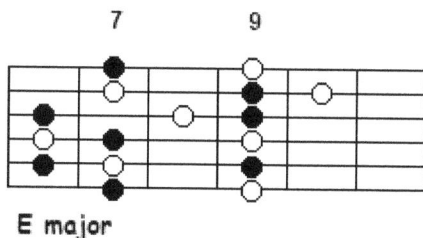

E major

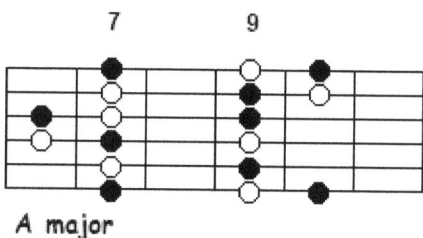

A major

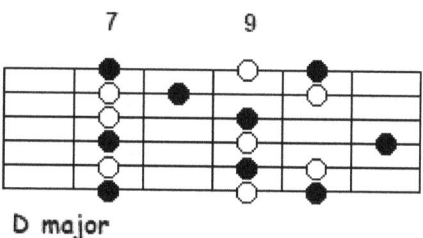

D major

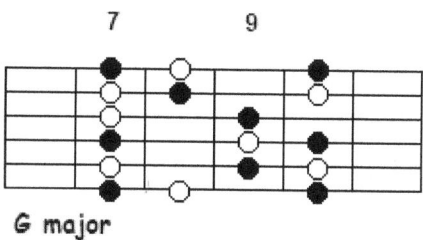

G major

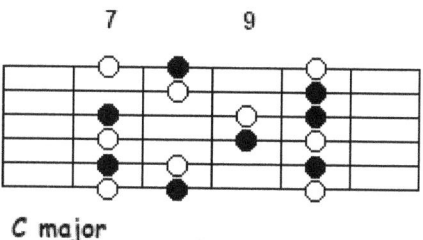

C major

Notice how patterns emerge. Once again, for simplicity, we'll look at a pattern beginning on the first two strings and see how it appears across the neck in that position. The note on the sixth fret in the D major map doesn't appear in the map as we've learned it, but that's where your knowledge of the notes on your guitar neck will help you see these possibilities. You'll discover all kinds of other ways to approach things as you understand the overall concept of MAS4JI and get comfortable with it.

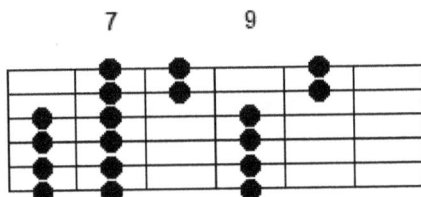

The next example will use a three-string pattern I developed from the major maps that uses note skipping for an intervallic approach so I can get some interesting "fake" dissonance while playing right in the pocket over the chords. It's related to the major maps we just examined above.

It's also very helpful to play through the cycle using the altered and major map pairs together because those come in handy in certain situations and it gives you more options to play with tension and resolution in slower moving cycle progressions or imply them in droning vamps. So you could play the C# altered and F# major maps in position and move to the F# altered and B major maps, followed by the B altered and E major, the E altered and A major, and so on right through all twelve keys.

Sometimes you might encounter a cycle progression where the I is played as a dominant to create added tension and delay resolution, faking out the listener. For example, you might find F#7-B7-E7-A7-Amaj7. When you reach the A7, you can use the A altered map for, then resolve to the A major map over the Amaj7. If the A7 is played very briefly, like a passing chord for only a couple beats, you can ignore it and just use the A major map, which will clash for a moment, creating some tension, before resolving into the Amaj7. If the chord lingers a little, you could even play the D major map (for the Mixolydian sound) and then resolve to the A major map.

Other avenues to explore in that situation would be to play the A map with side-slipping or with the tri-tone slip . . . or a mix of both. And you can always throw in some chromatic tones too. What matters is that you confidently play strong rhythmic and melodic lines that resolve. You want to be an aural gymnast that pulls off a feat and lands on your feet. Don't forget to take a bow.

To sum things up, jazz progressions can get a little complicated. When learning a tune, examine its form so you can plan a strategy and pair up the maps you need, then practice them until you're comfortable freely improvising lines over the progressions. Patterns are very helpful and work really well to get you started, but you can also play with the maps using all the ideas we've learned throughout this book.

Fragments of the maps in combination with those techniques will almost *always* produce great results and you'll find yourself quickly gravitating toward ideas you like as you develop your own style and approach using the Master Improvisation System for Jazz Improvisation. Adopt and adapt.

Chapter Ten: Going Solo

It's time to go solo. This chapter helps us apply everything we've learned in this book to navigate a basic 12 bar jazz blues in A major. This is where the rubber hits the road.

Strategies

When we're playing and it comes time to solo, we don't just completely wing it and start playing any notes right off the cuff without a game plan. That's just asking for a train wreck unless you have a phenomenal ear and incredible talent. Musicians thoroughly learn a piece of music inside and out and usually live with that music for some time before they ever hit the stage with it. Not only must we learn the melody (head) and the harmony, we have to study the piece and develop strategies for soloing on the progression so when it comes time to play, you're ready to hit the ground running with ideas.

Frequently, you'll learn from a lead sheet which includes the chords. In fact, the solo section could look just like the chord chart below. Sometimes it might include the melody, while at other times you might just have a simple chord chart like below. The chords are often simple like the ones here and you're left to add extensions (9,11,13) or alterations (b9,#9,b5,#5), depending on what the and tune requires and according to personal style and taste..

These additions can become very important for choosing which maps to use over them. For extensions, it's often safest to use the major map, although it's possible to blow over a quick chord that only lasts a couple beats with the altered map as easily as it is to use a lot of chromatic notes. It's all about where you're going, so watch what's coming up and plan how you're going to get there and where you're going to resolve your ideas. Music is like telling a story and you want to use coherent sentences and make concise statements, even when they're a little radical. Twists and turns in the plot can make for a fun ride.

Sometimes you may hear chords like the Ab7 in measures 6 and 7 that are not a part of the song's harmony and just fly by quickly. Those are passing chords and you can just ignore them and blow over them. They're simply adding some momentum to the comping and are still pulling toward where the harmony is actually going. Some musicians use them sparingly, others use them a little more frequently, and some don't bother with them at all. I just included one here and wrote it in for demonstration.

A7   Bm7   Fm7   Bb7   A7   A6   Cm7   F7

E7   F#m7 B7   E7   Ab7   A7 A7sus   Ab7   G7   C7

Bm7   E7   C#7   F#7   B7   E7

You can grab a pen, pencil or marker and write on the lead sheet or you can print a copy, but it's a good idea to have something you can mark up. It's helpful to analyze the progression with Roman numerals and the basic functions the chords are playing in the progression, such as their role as a secondary dominant (a 7th chord that's not resolving, like the I7, which we might expect to be a Imaj7), a substitute ii-V, tritone substitution (bII or even a tritone ii-V, like I use a couple times here). Write this information on the lead sheet. Mark that baby up!

Next, we figure out what maps we can use for each chord, measure or even multiple measures in jazz tunes with a harmony that moves slower through the changes. Write the maps in wherever you feel comfortable. I put them just below the staff in the example below. Looking at the first measure, I have an A7 and Bm7. Bm7-A7 is a ii-V in D major, so I choose that as my more "inside" option. It will be the "safer" option, less dissonant. It will depend more on chromatic strategies if I want to introduce more dissonance. A altered is my more "outside" option if I want to go for a more contemporary sound with more dissonance in the line without depending much on chromaticism.

The line doesn't resolve to D major, but instead goes to a tritone sub of Fm7-Bb7 leading to a temporary resolution of A7-A6, with A6 being the close relative of Amaj7. I chose E altered for the for the tritone sub and bring things to a relative resolution with D major because A7 is the V chord of that key and our I chord in the jazz blues is a dominant chord. A major is not my best choice, but D major is enharmonic with A Mixolydian.

Now you might see how we can easily overthink with improvising. This is the behind-the-scenes grunt work that will prepare us for improvising freely when the time comes. The key is to simplify the progression and find key centers then match those to maps that we can pair up and start using over the progression. Once we pair them up, we play them together as we've been doing until we can move freely between them, frontwards, backwards, inside out and upside down. So we want to be able to use that D major and E altered (or A and E altered pair) comfortably up and down the neck, then know how to move that E altered into D major.

One thing that can make things easier when first planning things is pairing up the maps you find comfortable playing, where you get a lot of melodic ideas, and which are on areas of the neck you gravitate toward. Practice improvising there and expand out naturally as you get more comfortable and are ready to reach further and cover more area. The maps are always the same and pairing them up gets easier and easier as you move forward. Also, you can use all of this with your three-notes-per-string scales, favorite licks and arpeggios wherever you like because everything fits together and helps you develop your personal style.

It seems like a lot, but after a little while you'll find that a lot of the progressions in more traditional tonal jazz have repetitive movements that happen frequently and these recurring harmonic themes will become easier and easier to navigate as you build your repertoire. Of course, all of this is even easier if you're just looking to incorporate jazz sounds in your own genre and style. Although we're looking at some jazz blues. all of this equally applies to developing strategies for Rhythm Changes and any other chord progressions you'll encounter in traditional jazz. Study the rest of the chord chart to see how I've arrived at my map options.

A7	Bm7	Fm7	Bb7	A7	A6	Cm7	F7
I7	ii	(tritone ii-V)		I7		(tritone ii-V)	

D major
A altered   E altered   D major   B altered

E7	F#m7 B7	E7		(Ab7)	A7 A7sus	(Ab7)	G7	C7
V7	(ii-V)	V7			I7		(tritone II7-V7)	

A major   E major   A major   D major   F# altered
E altered B altered E altered

Bm7	E7	A7	F#7	B7	E7
ii	V7	I7	VI7	II7	V7

A major   A major   D major   B major   E major   A major
           E altered F# altered   E altered

For the solo transcription, I've included the maps I specifically use to solo over the progression. For the progression itself, I've kept the voices of the chords super simple, using just the guide tone voices of the 7th and 3rd. This keeps things more open so I can use either a major or altered map over many measures . . . or I can even mix the two, although I don't do that here. Notice how I sometimes ignore a chord in the measure and just blow over it. This is far from an uncommon practice in jazz, especially with a fast-moving harmony, like bebop. Just make sure you're making strong melodic statements and playing toward points of resolution (or relative resolution) with strong, finished ideas that sound complete.

It's very important to play lines that make sense melodically and rhythmically. A strong statement will cover a lot of ground and make "wrong" things sound right. This is why some advanced musicians will even superimpose one key over another in various ways and still sound great. Jazz has some loose "rules," but it's is also about breaking the rules. Every time a style or sound in jazz gets firmly established, someone comes along and throws a monkey wrench in the machine to mix things up and keep it fresh.

There are many tools we can use to make great lines. For one, use a healthy mixture of everything we've learned here: portions of the maps as arpeggios and triads out of order and skipping, quartal arpeggios, 3/4 and 4/3 triads, the pentatonics within, black & white (scalar) playing, side-slipping and tritone slipping, and chromaticism. Very useful techniques include using rhythmic and melodic motifs, which I use plenty of in the solo because they're like a glue that holds things together. I also use call and response lines, which give the lines a conversational quality, in keeping with the idea of telling a story.

Also, I don't just jump all over the neck of the guitar randomly. I explore areas of the neck before moving on. I often begin a line a half step away from where one just ended or on a note shared by two maps, which helps things flow smoothly and keeps them connected. I move to a new area on the neck when it feels right. There are no hard and fast rules, so explore and use your ear to guide your fingers and let the notes follow; the music will do the talking.

For the solo, I mark the approach and passing tones with a + sign and acknowledge other ideas with brackets, such as enclosures or side-slipping. I leave it up to you to notice arpeggios and triads and what I'm doing with those, as well as pentatonic and quartal ideas. Since I've indicated what maps I'm using, it shouldn't be too hard to see where I'm getting my ideas. I'm not overthinking things, like what I'm superimposing, what voice leading, guide tone lines or target notes I'm using. I'm just using the maps to create lines while focusing on playing musical ideas. Pairing the maps takes care of those other things for me so I can "play more and think later," especially because I got all the thinking out of the way earlier and prepared myself for improvising over the changes.

So, let's go solo!

A7 Bm7 Fm7 Bb7 A7 A6
Bar 1
D major
E altered
D major
Cm7 F7 E7 F#m7 B7 E7 (Ab7)
Bar 4
B altered
A major
A major
side-slipping
A7 A7sus A7 (Ab7) G7 C7 Bm7
Bar 7
D major
side-slilpping
F# altered
A major
E7 A7 F#7 B7
Bar 10
A major
B major
E major

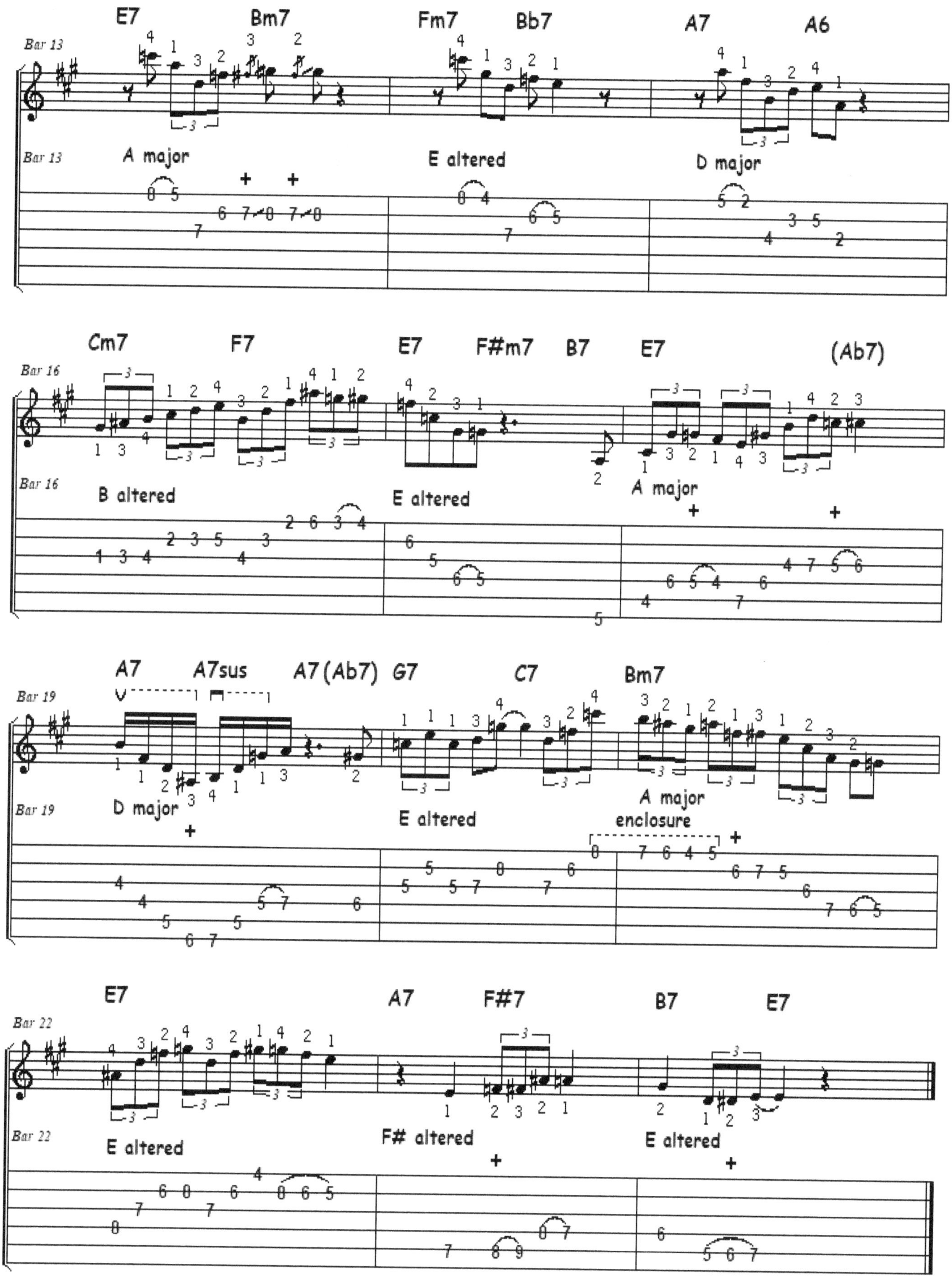
Bar 13
E7 Bm7 Fm7 Bb7 A7 A6
A major
E altered
D major
Bar 16
Cm7 F7 E7 F#m7 B7 E7 (Ab7)
B altered
E altered
A major
Bar 19
A7 A7sus A7 (Ab7) G7 C7 Bm7
D major
E altered
A major
enclosure
Bar 22
E7 A7 F#7 B7 E7
E altered
F# altered
E altered

That's it! Again, I take ideas and recycle them melodically and rhythmically in different places, repurposing them to keep common threads throughout the solo. A particularly great way to do this is to embellish the song's melody, manipulating the rhythm, and developing it in various ways. Thelonious Monk was a master at this approach and you'll hear many jazz artists do this in their solos. It's a great way to tie your solo into the song, which is the greater story your solo is playing a role in.

Have fun exploring the endless possibilities and using the Master Arpeggio System for both improvisation and composition. It's a powerful tool once everything comes together and you're finally off the ground and flying free.

Conclusion

Thanks for taking this interesting journey. It's all about the tension and release, following the chord progressions, and playing toward points of resolution. We've focused on the ii-V-I because it's at the core of the jazz sound much like the I-IV-V is at the core of the blues. Common substitutions like the bII tri-tone and the secondary dominant and ii-V cycles are also tricky moves you'll encounter regularly in jazz.

I hope this method is helpful and makes things a little clearer, giving you a common core that will ground you while helping you take off and fly free at the same time by putting the seemingly complex language of improvising cool jazz-style lines at your fingertips.

The best teacher for jazz harmony is simply learning jazz standards. However, it might be helpful to do some extra research and study chord construction, shell voicings, extensions and alterations, chord substitutions, quartal harmony and jazz progressions, along with reharmonization. Online resources are plentiful, especially on YouTube.

If you've enjoyed this book but still have some questions about what's next because you still hear so many other sounds in jazz and fusion that aren't covered here, there's more. MAS4JI will continue with **The Master Arpeggio System for Jazz Improvisation: Minor & More.** It will introduce seven new master arpeggios that have a significantly shorter learning curve, then we'll explore playing over common jazz turnarounds and apply everything we've learned in both books in a 24 bar solo over a 12 bar jazz blues. MAS4JI: M&M ties everything together and prepares you to play over complete jazz forms.

See you soon.

About the Author

Dennis Roberts started his musical journey in his mid-teens as a self-taught guitarist playing hard rock and heavy metal, but was always very interested in studying music theory and playing techniques. It wasn't until his mid-30s that he went to college and formally studied music theory, performance, and recording, also delving into some classical while focusing mainly on jazz, a style he's been listening to since childhood. Dennis graduated with honors and continues to pursue his music passions.